EBURY PRESS

THE KARGIL GIRL

Flight Lieutenant Gunjan Saxena (retd) is the first female Indian Air Force (IAF) officer to serve in the war zone. Long before the first female fighter pilots were commissioned into the IAF, she made history by flying a Cheetah helicopter in the Kargil War and rescuing several soldiers. Saxena was inspired to join the IAF by her father, who served in the Indian Army. As part of the family legacy, she decided to join the armed forces after completing her graduation from Delhi University's Hansraj College. In 1994, she cleared her Services Selection Board (SSB) interview and joined the Air Force Academy in Dundigal. When the Kargil War broke out in 1999, she helped turn things in India's favour, becoming one of the first women on the front line.

Kiran Nirvan is the pseudonym used by authors Kirandeep Singh and Nirvan Singh. Together they have authored two bestselling books—*Nasteya: The Aryan Saga* and *21 Kesaris: The Untold Story of the Battle of Saragarhi*. The latter inspired the Akshay Kumar-starrer *Kesari*. Kirandeep Singh is the former head of the department of management studies, Global Institutes, Amritsar, and is currently pursuing his doctorate in the discipline. He began exploring his passion for writing in his teenage years and has authored more than a hundred poems, short stories, novels, song lyrics and couplets in both English and Punjabi. Nirvan Singh is a serving officer in the Indian Army, while also being an avid artist, writer and adventurer. It is his endeavour to write the stories of grit and determination, wisdom and valour, of men and women from the Indian armed forces, and other exemplary individuals of this nation.

ALSO BY KIRAN NIRVAN

21 Kesaris: The Untold Story of the Battle of Saragarhi
Nasteya: The Aryan Saga

THE
KARGIL
GIRL

An Autobiography

Flt Lt **Gunjan Saxena** (retd)
with **Kiran Nirvan**

EBURY
PRESS

An imprint of Penguin Random House

EBURY PRESS

USA | Canada | UK | Ireland | Australia
New Zealand | India | South Africa | China

Ebury Press is part of the Penguin Random House group of companies
whose addresses can be found at global.penguinrandomhouse.com

Published by Penguin Random House India Pvt. Ltd
7th Floor, Infinity Tower C, DLF Cyber City,
Gurgaon 122 002, Haryana, India

Penguin
Random House
India

First published in Ebury Press by Penguin Random House India 2020

ISBN 9780143451068

Typeset in Adobe Garamond Pro by Manipal Technologies Limited, Manipal
Printed at Thomson Press India Ltd, New Delhi

www.penguin.co.in

To the heroes of the Kargil conflict
&
To this nation's men and women in uniform,
serving and retired

FOREWORD

At the outset, I would like to congratulate Flight Lieutenant Gunjan Saxena (retd) for writing her autobiography, as she has been a pathbreaker in her field! Being among the first few women officers who were given commission in the Flying Branch, she fought an uphill battle to break the stereotype of an Indian woman! Being part of the second course of women officers selected for helicopter-flying, she was assigned to a Cheetah/Chetak (Alouette III) unit in Udhampur, whose primary task was forward air control, which was to fly in the thick of combat during the erstwhile close air support/battlefield air strike (BAS) missions and visually guiding fighter aircraft to their targets.

In her book, Gunjan has successfully explained what it takes to become an officer in the Indian Air Force.

Her retelling of the Kargil War made me go down memory lane and reminded me of my own experience in the war, wherein I was commanding 17 Squadron (Golden Arrows), where we worked closely with 132 FAC flight for all our BAS missions in the Kashmir Valley. During the Kargil conflict, as the main mode of attack had shifted to GPS-aided bombing from the classic BAS, Gunjan's unit provided vital information about where our bombs were dropping relative to the target.

Post the ceasefire of sorts, her task was to carry me and the commanding officer of 108 Squadron for a recce sortie of the target area and a visit to 3 and 8 Division Headquarters at their operational locations. I was pleasantly surprised to see a calm and confident lady officer toting an AK-47 as her weapon in the Cheetah helicopter! In Kargil, I also happened to meet her brother Captain Anshuman Saxena of the Army Ordnance Corps. I asked them if their parents were on tenterhooks as both their children were deployed in the battle zone! The answer was a nonchalant no!

Later, she would earn the rightful title of 'The Kargil Girl', the first female Indian Air Force officers to serve in the battle zone. The Indian Air Force definitely needs more women officers like her, who can inspire young girls to dream of being combatants and serving their country.

I wish Gunjan and Kiran Nirvan the very best in their endeavour. I am sure this book will serve as an inspiration to future generations and for all those who aim to conquer the blue skies.

Jai Hind!

—Air Chief Marshal Birender Singh Dhanoa
PVSM, AVSM, YSM, VM (retd)
25th Chief of Air Staff of the Indian Air Force

ONE

July 1994

Do I really have it in me? I asked myself almost inaudibly. A strange silence fell over me as I stared at my reflection in the glass window of the AC coach. My train to Mysore had just arrived, and I was supposed to board soon.

Am I worthy of becoming an officer in the Indian armed forces? I asked myself, looking at my reflection, unmoving. Even the PA announcement by the railway station staff failed to distract me. Beads of sweat collected on my face and at the back of my neck. Whether it was my body's mechanism of cooling itself down on a hot July afternoon, or just me perspiring out of nervousness, I could not tell. We had been waiting for the train at the platform in the scorching heat for an hour, and it may have well been the weather of Chennai. But then again, the opportunity that I had been eagerly waiting for was just hours away, so it could very well have been nervousness, after all.

'The train will leave in five minutes.' It was my father's voice that pulled me back to reality. All of a sudden, discreet chatter, PA announcements, the incessant hollering of hawkers, the train's honking, the sound of a radio somewhere playing the title track from *Hum Aapke Hain Kaun* filled the air. In this country, railway stations have always been crowded and busy. I turned to look at my father. His handlebar moustache, a style he had sported back when I was a child, had given way to a simple chevron above his thin lips over the years. I could not recollect if it had been a sudden and deliberate change, or merely a trick of age. It still added to the overall charm of his long, chiselled face. His round black eyes had sunk deeper now and his face looked more weather-beaten than I remembered. Drops of sweat had settled on the contours of his long, straight nose and above his thin, stretched brows. There were two or more wrinkles under his chin that I hadn't spotted earlier. Even when his moderately long hair, swept back on his head, and the shorter hair on the sides, wasn't entirely black any more, there was no change in his commanding personality as he stood tall in front of me.

Dark patches of sweat had formed on his khaki shirt, which he was wearing with black bell-bottomed trousers, but he seemed as excited as he had been on the day I had received a call letter for the SSB (Services Selection Board). I remember how he had jumped up in excitement and hugged me. I remember how he had marked the dates on the calendar and noted instructions mentioned in the letter in his pocket diary. I remember how he had rushed to Avadi railway station to book a ticket for me to Mysore, how he had carefully collected items I would require for my SSB exam, how he had ensured I had packed everything according to the checklist. To me, getting recommended in the SSB meant a chance at a glorious career. To him, it was validation of his relentless efforts in bringing me up the way he had. To make sure I would not miss my train, he had rung up the railway enquiry office every few minutes that morning to confirm whether the train was on time. Back in those days, we did not have the luxury of checking a train's running status on the Internet. It was an analogue world, crisscrossed with wires and cables; the label 'wireless' was still struggling to find its place. And I was struggling to hide my nervousness from Papaji.

'You seem worried, Gunju, but remember what I've always told you, all these twenty years of your life,' he said, as he pulled a handkerchief from his pocket, wiping the beads of sweat off my face. 'Just be who you are. No pretence, no false answers to the interviewer's questions—just be Gunjan Saxena.'

'I'll remember, Papaji, and I'll also remember that I'm the daughter of Lieutenant Colonel Anup Kumar Saxena.'

Papaji was a commissioned officer in the Corps of EME in the Indian Army. I looked up at him and smiled as I playfully gestured a salute. Standing next to the bogie's door, my mother smiled. She was smartly dressed in a printed white suit with a plain white dupatta that day. As always, she wore a big, round, crimson bindi, placed perfectly between her pencil-thin, bristly brows. I could see a few wrinkles on the sides of her warm, expressive, beautiful eyes. Her coal-black, wavy hair, that had once cascaded down her back, was now tied in a bun at the nape of her neck. There was no outburst of emotions, no melodramatic moments, just her signature smile. And I knew how worried she was. I was travelling all by myself, and that too, for my first SSB. But she always chose to appear strong, rather than to exhibit her worries. When I had to leave home for the first time to join Hansraj College in Delhi, where I was supposed to pursue my BSc in anthropology, my brother was so worried that he argued with my parents to not let me go and my father lectured for hours before I left—but my mother, Mrs Kirti Saxena, didn't react. She just smiled and wished me strength and luck. She didn't cry that day; neither did she let me cry. No wonder she is the most composed in a family of short-tempered siblings and father . . . and a couple of crazy dogs.

They walked me to my seat. Lieutenant Colonel Anshuman Saxena, my year-and-four-month-older sibling whom I called Dada, had carefully tucked my suitcase underneath the seat and secured it to the frame with a steel chain. It was more of a ritual when travelling in Indian trains than a safety measure.

'You take care of yourself, Gunjan,' Dada said, looking at the two teenage boys sitting in front of my seat from the corner of his eye, and then continued loudly, 'even though my seat is in the adjacent bogie, I'll keep coming to check on you.' He punctuated every word with his index finger, ending with a wink. I nodded, even though I knew he was bluffing. It was just meant to be a statutory warning of sorts, but not for me. Dada had always acted older than his age when it came to being the elder brother. Tall and handsome, he was dressed in a check shirt tucked neatly into his jeans, as he stood next to me. There was a grimace on his thin, chiselled face as his eyes scanned the bogie. To him, his little sister would always be immature and inexperienced, but he wouldn't counsel her, he wouldn't express his concerns—he would simply threaten those he thought meant her harm, even if they actually didn't.

The train horn blew for the last time, signalling its departure. Maa and Dada said their goodbyes and left. But Papaji stayed on. 'I haven't even prepared for the SSB, Papaji. I feel like I'm on the edge here,' I said.

'That's where you belong . . . on the edge . . . since you were a child,' he gently cupped my chin in his battle-hardened hands and looked as if reminiscing. Then, after a pause, he said, 'Besides, no preparations are required for things that are meant to be . . .'

I was just another girl before I became Flight Lieutenant Gunjan Saxena, before I actively took part in the 1999 Kargil War, where India emerged victorious in the face of heavy odds, before I was felicitated with the Shaurya Vir Puraskar by the Uttar Pradesh government, before I came to be known as the 'Kargil Girl'. I was just another girl with dreams in her eyes and passion in her heart, clueless on board the train that would take her on the journey of her lifetime. Shortlisted for the SSB for the 4th Short Service Commission for Women pilot course in 1994, I was both nervous and excited as the train journey commenced—excited because I had grown up dreaming of wearing the uniform my father wore, and nervous because I was about to appear for the SSB interview, unprepared. Of the thirteen SSBs across India,

I was selected to appear for the one in Mysore, which was primarily for shortlisted candidates for the Indian Air Force. All I knew about SSB was that it would evaluate my suitability for becoming an officer using a standardized protocol evaluation system, which comprises personality and intelligence tests, both written and practical-task-based, and interviews, and that the evaluation process would take five to six days. The evaluation would be to determine whether or not I possessed the fifteen officer-like qualities, or OLQs, required to become an officer. When we talk about OLQs, we talk about effective intelligence, reasoning ability, power of expression, self-confidence, determination, organizing ability, initiative, courage, cooperation, a sense of responsibility, stamina, group influencing ability, liveliness, social adaptability and speed of decision: qualities that an officer must have in order to lead men into battle, some of which can be gained through day-to-day experiences and learning, while others must be naturally present, inherited or imbibed. A number of SSB training centres groom thousands of defence aspirants to effectively perform in SSB. But I had never visited any. I couldn't help but think of how the other candidates appearing with me might have either had prior experience of SSB interviews or training from some institute, which would narrow down my chances of being recommended.

I had never wondered if I possessed those OLQs until I boarded the train. What does a twenty-year-old girl, who had just waded through the toughest and most confusing years of life, know about it anyway? Self-introspection is not meant to be in the nature of the young and the restless—they are meant to make mistakes, fall, rise, experience and learn, before they are finally old enough to sit back and pass verdict on their younger selves. And I was still quite young, and a lot more restless. But the whole SSB thing and Papaji's words triggered a downpour of memories and I couldn't help but think about what my parents had always told me—that I was different. They would back this up with memories and events from even before I was born. *That's where you belong . . . on the edge.*

The year 1974 was an eventful one in India's history. Under Project Smiling Buddha, India had successfully conducted its first nuclear test in the Thar desert, workers of the Indian Railways had created history with the largest industrial strike recorded in the world, and there was an outbreak of smallpox in Bihar, Orissa (now Odisha) and West Bengal. And somewhere in the army cantonment of Guwahati in Assam, Mrs Kirti Saxena, mother-to-be, had just survived eight months with a swollen belly. After going through nausea and vomiting, fatigue, backache and headache for endless days and nights, she watched with a sense of delight as her second child entered the world. Captain Anup Kumar Saxena made sure he was available to tend to all the needs and demands of his pregnant wife as best he could. He had liaised with the cantonment's administrative officer and gotten accommodation that was close to the Military Hospital in Narangi. He had stocked the refrigerator with his wife's favourite food items; a timetable for regular medical check-ups and medicines was scribbled into his diary. It was not only his wife who formed the epicentre of his concerns. He yearned for a girl this time, a girl he would raise the way he wished to. His mother, my grandmother, had not let him have his way with the first child. She did not believe in modern parenting techniques. But he was hell-bent on raising his second child the way he thought right, and to make sure he succeeded in his mission, he spent hours reading Dr Benjamin Spock's books on parenting to understand the physical and emotional aspects of a child and the dynamics of a family. This, however, was opposed by his orthodox mother again, but this time, he would just not listen.

Mrs Saxena, my mother, entered the ninth month of her pregnancy in the last week of August 1974. There had been a pinkish glow on her face for weeks. 'She's eager to come out now,' Papaji commented when my mother told him the baby had just kicked.

'She? Why not he?' she teased him, gazing out at rain-washed trees from their bedroom's window. 'Mother is not going to approve of your friend Spock's advice,' Maa said. 'Do you think she'll allow us to have a different room for the baby?'

'I'll not argue with her this time,' a determined Papaji replied.

'You know her temperament,' Maa said.

'And you can take care of it—like you always do,' Papaji retorted.

'Okay . . . Okay . . . I'll try,' she said, and continued in a murmur, 'dealing with everyone's temperament seems to be my only job in this house.'

'Did you say something?'

A sudden rush of pain changed her facial expressions. 'The baby's coming,' Maa said. She grabbed her belly and stood up.

'I told you she's eager.' He didn't look at her until she screamed and said, 'She's coming NOW!'

The ambulance ride to the Military Hospital in Narangi was a very nervous one for Papaji. He knew Maa was in a lot of pain, even though she tried her best not to show it.

He knew there was nothing he could do except be by her side. 'You're a strong woman,' he kept encouraging her. The hospital staff took Maa inside the labour room as Papaji's friend, the army doctor, arrived. Five intense hours passed as a worried Papaji waited outside. He nervously paced the corridor, sweat covering his crew-cut hair and moustache. He prayed with each passing minute and waited. He didn't even notice when my grandmother and little Dada arrived. Then came the moment he was longing for. The doctor came out of the room and Papaji paused mid-stride. 'Congratulations, Captain,' the doctor said cheerfully.

'Is it a girl?' Papaji waited for his reply.

'It's a boy,' the doctor said, shaking his hand.

Papaji took a moment, and smiled only customarily before he replied plainly, 'It's okay . . . I'll try again for a girl.'

At this the doctor burst into laughter, hugged Papaji, patted his back and said, 'No need to try again . . . It's a girl.' On hearing this, Papaji smiled and hugged him back, blinked away his tears and then hurried into the labour room . . .

Captain Saxena and his wife spent the next few weeks tending to my needs. They took turns to look after both the kids. Grandmother was a big help in those days. Papaji implemented Dr Spock's suggestions despite Grandmother's protests. He made me sleep in a separate room, inside a crate, after a few months had passed. He kept their bedroom door open in case I cried in the middle of the night, which I'm sure I did quite often. At times, Dada pushed my pram and took me to either Maa or Papaji when I cried. In such instances, Papaji would proudly say to my grandmother, 'See how Anshu is learning to take care of his sister when he cannot even speak yet. And you question *my* parenting.' He would not let these incidents go unnoticed. He would observe something about his children, something that he thought made them different from the others.

I was only six months old when Papaji started to teach me to sit. He would make me sit in the centre of the bed, and I would tumble forward and fall on one of the strategically placed cushions around. He would keep repeating this and I would keep falling. 'You enjoy it, don't you?' he would say to me and I would apparently chuckle. Of course, I didn't understand a word. But he was confused. Dada had started to balance himself when he was five months old. 'Maybe she's not ready yet,' Maa said from the corner of the room as she fed Dada in her lap.

'Maybe you're right,' he replied, gently placing me on the edge of the bed and reaching for a glass of water kept on the other side. As he drank from his glass, he noticed something that he would recount on multiple occasions when I had grown up. Twenty odd seconds had passed and I was still sitting straight on the edge of the bed. A minute passed and I was still sitting. Papaji's eyes brightened and he exclaimed proudly, 'Our daughter doesn't belong to the comfort zone!' He gleefully looked at my mother and said, 'She likes being on the edge.'

* * *

'I think you should go wake your brother. He hasn't come yet,' the boy sitting in front of my seat said. It was the first and the last time he'd speak to me. The train halted at Mysore railway station and I unlocked my luggage from underneath my seat.

'He's not on this train,' I told him and started to walk towards the exit while he sat there, confused. It was a pleasant afternoon and the road outside the railway station was still wet from the morning drizzle. The air was moist but not as warm as it used to be back home. As I boarded a taxi for the SSB centre, I couldn't help but think about how my father had cherished every moment he had spent with me when I was a child. In those moments, he learnt things about me that he would later talk about, things that he believed made me different; it helped me in ways I had not understood until then. But during this train journey, I began to understand how his unwavering faith in me was finally going to help. It was only when the taxi dropped me outside the centre, where hundreds of female candidates stood and waited with their luggage by their side, that I suddenly found myself shrinking in size as I stood silent in the middle of these unknown faces, all of whom were gawking at me . . . judging me . . .

What now, Gunjan Saxena, what now?

TWO

Getting out of the taxi was easy, but standing silent in the middle of a group of unknown girls was not. At first, the only thing I noticed was a swarm of shortlisted candidates—250 unknown faces—many of whom would have to go home on the first day of the interview itself, right after the screening. There was an uncertainty looming over this nervous crowd, including me. *Would I be one of them?* I shrugged away any negative feelings and got into one of the queues for the initial documentation. Tables were set up by air force personnel in uniform, outside a big iron gate of the Air Force Selection Board in CV Complex, Sidharth Nagar, Mysore.

'Which institute are you from?' A tall, dusky, skinny girl with short hair asked as she patted my shoulder.

She was the first person to speak to me since I had landed at the gates of the centre.

'Excuse me?' I turned to look at her.

'Look over there,' she said in a south Indian accent. My gaze followed her finger, pointing towards the first queue from the right. 'That bunch of well-suited girls wearing similar-coloured T-shirts and already pretending to be officers are from "Excel" SSB training centre.' She was blunt but right. Unlike us, standing in our pyjamas and still weary from a long journey, those five–six candidates were dressed in light yellow T-shirts buttoned up to their necks and neatly tucked inside their white shorts, with their institute's logo written on the back of their shirts. With their hands interlocked behind their backs, chins up and chests out, they were whispering to each other, passing judgmental stares at the likes of us.

'Maybe this is what these training centres do,' I added, 'they teach them how to act like officers.'

'Act? Or pretend?' the south Indian girl commented.

'You cannot pretend to be someone you're not, whatever your training,' I said.

'Correct. And if I was the interviewer, I'd give them a negative ten for the colour of their T-shirts alone,' she said, and both of us chuckled. Unlike me, she appeared jovial and happy.

'But you cannot rule out the fact that someone might be genuine among them,' I said, to which she rolled her eyes in disagreement.

'By the way, I'm Gunjan. And I'm not from any institute.'

'I'm Hema Rajkumar. And likewise.' She extended her hand and I shook it. 'Also, I'm starving. Are they going to give us food?'

'Lunch has been arranged. It's written in the joining instructions,' I said. It was then that it dawned on me that after the lunch, the first test would be conducted. The feeble smile that Hema had managed to bring on my face vanished, along with the little hunger I had earlier felt. I had this feeling that I wasn't prepared. If that wasn't all, I now knew I would be competing against candidates from reputed training institutes.

The Indian Air Force personnel, a corporal and a sergeant, let us in after they checked our documents and allotted us a 'chest number' each—a number printed on a square piece of apron-like cloth that candidates would wear during tests. It was to be our only identity until the SSB interview concluded. I was allotted 'Chest Number 04'. As we entered the gates, a squad of some thirty male candidates with similar chest numbers from another ongoing SSB interview in the same centre hurried past us. They hardly noticed us. The air inside the centre seemed intense, and it was eerily quiet, haunted by the ghosts of the thousands of dreams that had died here. But in some other places, like the vast garden in front of a white office building with sky-blue borders, the barracks and the ante room, and the small cafeteria next to an STD booth, the joy of recommendation lurked. Many air warriors who ruled the skies must have overcome their first hurdles in this very place.

'Good afternoon, candidates. I'm Squadron Leader Manoj Yadav and I'll be coordinating the day's events. If you're done chatting, please get yourselves arranged in twenty-five rows of ten candidates each,' Squadron Leader Manoj Yadav, a medium-built, fair-skinned officer with a sharp crew-cut hairstyle, dressed in a finely creased uniform, announced from the front of the crowd and the chit-chatting died away. Slowly, the girls shifted as per this young officer's strict command, loud enough to have been heard by all of us. Many gawked at him in silence.

'How handsome!' Hema whispered in my ear. 'God, please get me through the screening if he's going to be our coordinating officer.'

'If that's where your focus is right now,' I added, 'you really need God's help.'

'I can't think straight, Gunjan, I'm hungry.'

As we chuckled at Hema's nonsensical correlation, the officer shifted his gaze and stared at us. Caught and confused, we tried to look away but it was too late.

'What are you two so happy about?' he asked plainly. Neither of us responded. 'I'll see which one of you is still smiling after the aptitude test is over.'

At lunch, I hardly ate, as compared to Hema. I wasn't smiling when we entered the examination hall later in the afternoon. I just felt quiet and confused. I had not practised for the aptitude test. Papaji had told me it would be easy and that I was smart enough to make it through. But the nervousness inside the examination hall and on the face of fellow candidates had suddenly made this test a fearsome affair. I began to doubt myself. *But aptitude is only basic IQ, Gunjan*—Papaji's words reverberated in my head. What made him think I was smart enough for this test? Was it a fair judgement or merely a father's love for his little girl? Only the question paper would tell. And then I waited . . .

* * *

February 1975

It had been six months since my parents had had a good night's sleep—six long and weary months, with the nights as laborious as the days spent changing diapers and tending to the needs of two little ones about the house. Little Anshuman missed his grandmother, who had gone back to Badaun, Uttar Pradesh, in the first week of January, since Guwahati's humid winters had become unbearable for her aching joints. Papaji and Maa missed her too. She had been a helping hand in taking care of Dada while I continued to raise hell with my periodic cries and untimely demands to be fed. But one fine night in February, I slept throughout, bringing some much-needed respite to Papaji and Maa.

'Are these dark circles under my eyes?' asked Maa. For the first time in a while she had found some time to herself. And Papaji could finally rip open the old radio whose dial had started to jam. It was half-past-six in the morning.

'Signs of insomnia,' Papaji said as he unscrewed the components of the radio.

'How strange,' Maa added, 'we have time now, but no sleep. Anshuman at least wore away the nights peacefully.'

'Don't blame my little Gunju,' my father said, still busy with the screwdriver. 'She'll make us proud one day, you'll see.'

'Of course she will,' my mother said, smiling. Papaji adjusted the dial, and after some indiscreet noise, the radio played the song *Karvatein Badalte Rahe Saari Raat Hum* (I kept twisting and turning all night long). As if on cue, Dada pulled my pram into the room with his little hands. I had begun to cry louder than the radio. Maa at once got out of bed and held me. Papaji ruffled Dada's hair and appreciated him for being responsible. Dada turned around and, still sleepy, crashed on their bed.

It had been a full hour since I had been crying in Maa's lap. All that rocking and feeding had been in vain. Papaji's efforts to divert my attention lasted for a few minutes before he became restless. The only unaffected person was Dada, who still slept as if on anaesthesia.

'Here, try this,' Papaji had come up with one last solution, something Maa had always been reluctant to try.

'No pacifier, please.' But even as Maa said this, Papaji put the pacifier between my lips. The tasteless, odourless pacifier worked its magic and I stopped crying at once. Papaji smiled, proud of his victory. 'She'll have buck teeth,' a worried Maa retorted.

'It's a myth,' Papaji replied as he looked at me and made funny faces.

'But everyone has been warning me.' Maa wouldn't let it go. Nevertheless, I was giggling, enjoying myself.

Papaji held me in his arms and replied, 'Everyone has their own opinion. It may not always be true. Many say it's not advisable to have a dog while there are infants in the house. But we'll still have one. Taking care of a dog teaches kids to be responsible. Don't worry about what everyone says.' As Papaji said this, he looked into my eyes and repeatedly motioned with his hand, a gesture of throwing the pacifier away. While Maa was still saying something,

I did something that startled both of them. I reached for the pacifier and, imitating Papaji's gesture, threw it away. They both looked at each other, quiet for a moment. Then Papaji picked up the pacifier and gave it to me again. I reached for it and, just like before, threw it away.

'What just happened?' Maa whispered.

'Our daughter just showed us she's so smart,' Papaji replied happily and looked at me. 'You're so smart, aren't you?'

'She agrees with you. She's a good follower,' Maa concluded optimistically.

'I can see that,' Papaji said as he planted a kiss on my forehead. 'But I want her to be a good leader too.'

* * *

Papaji would often share moments like these with me. It was as if he wanted to sow some kind of belief in me about myself, an anecdote that might help me when the time came. As I held the question paper of the aptitude test in my hands, I could clearly understand that the time had come. The test was all about applying skills to solve basic problems. I suddenly started to believe in my own ability to do exactly that. And what better time for self-introspection than a life-changing interview? Without fretting further, I began my test. It was time-based—ideally thirty seconds for each question. I raced against time and finished the test two minutes early and looked up. At a desk adjacent to mine, Hema's head was buried in the answer sheet but she, too, managed to finish in time. We sighed simultaneously as the examiner collected our answer sheets. Results were awaited eagerly.

The sun had crawled down the western sky as all the candidates waited in line outside the examination hall. There was a mild chill in the evening wind, which carried to us the faint aroma of dinner being cooked in the mess. Some girls passionately discussed the questions and their probable answers. Hema, however, was busy guessing the dinner menu with another girl, not really fretting like most of us. Restlessness threatened to get the better of me but I stood there as quietly as I could. As we heard Sqn Ldr Yadav's approaching footsteps, my heart began to thud in my chest. He held a file in his hand; inside it were the results. Multiple thoughts assaulted my mind at once. It must have been the same for all of us. We lined up quietly without the need for any instruction on seeing the coordinating officer standing in front of us. I didn't realize my legs were trembling.

'Good evening, candidates,' Sqn Ldr Yadav started to speak, 'I must tell you that all of you performed well, so it wasn't easy for us to make the selection.' I could hardly breathe as he continued. 'In this test, all of you are winners, but some of you have performed exceptionally well to meet our selection criteria. Those chest numbers that I will now announce are requested to please come and stand to my left.' And then he began calling out the numbers. 'Chest numbers 238, 236, 224, 208, 199, 197, 183 . . .' *God! Why did he have to start backwards?* I started to pick at my lower lip as I waited. After about a minute, I found myself standing in a bigger group as a smaller group continued to assemble to his left. *These had to be the ones who had made it through the screening.* As the chest numbers reached the double digits, I closed my eyes and saw a picture come to life in the darkness. It was Papaji, Maa and Dada smiling at me. For a moment, all other sounds ceased to exist.

'Chest number 04 . . . 04,' somebody from behind poked me and I opened my eyes at once. It was my chest number that had just been announced. I walked to Sqn Ldr Yadav's left at once, and his eyes followed me.

'That is all,' he announced.

But we still didn't know which of the two groups was the lucky one. One of us had to ask him. He replied, 'I will tell you after dinner; if I say anything now, most of you won't eat.'

'As if most of us can savour the meal happily now!' Hema, who also stood in the same group alongside me, said almost inaudibly.

An early dinner was served. Dinner tables turned into strategic sites for discussions among representatives from both groups, all hell-bent on deciphering the mystery of this unannounced half-result. I wasn't hungry any more. Or maybe I was, but I didn't feel like eating a thing! On the television in one corner of the dining hall, a news channel showed Sushmita Sen being crowned Miss Universe 1994. For as long as I sat there, I kept stirring the daal with my spoon, staring at her happy expressions.

We assembled on the same veranda in the two groups after dinner. Sqn Ldr Yadav arrived, dressed in mufti*. 'For the ones who didn't clear the test, arrangements for a night's stay are in place. You can leave tomorrow after breakfast. For those who already have reservations for tonight, a station bus will drop you to the railway station or the bus stop,' he announced. It was then that I realized that my father had not let me make reservations for the same day, afraid that he would jinx my chances with his presumption.

'Congratulations to the 105 candidates to my left,' Sqn Ldr Yadav turned to us and smiled. I let out a sigh

---

* Mufti, or civvies (slang for 'civilian attire'), refers to plain or ordinary clothes, especially when worn by someone who normally wears, or has long worn, a military or other uniform. 'Mufti' is a term used for casual dressing, as opposed to wearing a uniform.

of relief; I couldn't wait to share the news with Papaji. Some girls of our group let out a loud 'Yes!'. Some hugged each other. I shook hands with Hema and smiled. We had cleared the first obstacle.

THREE

'Whose photograph is that?' Hema asked as she buried her face inside my wide-open suitcase. Our beds were adjacent to each other inside the barracks and we had been asked to share the same luggage shelf.

'My father's photograph from his academy days,' I replied as I unpacked.

'He's in the army?' Hema asked. I nodded. I still hadn't informed Papaji that I had cleared the screening test.

'Why do you keep it?' a curious Hema asked.

'The same reason you keep your mother's old watch in your bag,' I replied.

'You noticed? How do you know it's my mother's?' a startled Hema asked.

'My mother had a similar one almost a decade ago. Besides, you kept it in your bag. You fear losing it and you don't wear it. So it's definitely not just a fashion statement,' I reasoned.

'That's *sakkath* [awesome],' she exclaimed, playfully hitting me.

It was half past eight and many of the girls who hadn't made it had already left for the railway station or the bus stand. Those who had made reservations for the next day were given a separate barracks, while the rest of us who were to stay on for the next five days were allotted eleven ten-bed barracks, their doors facing a square veranda, which had two badminton courts in each half of the square. The walls along the corridor were lined with framed photographs of heroes of the Indian Air Force and famous patriotic quotes. One such photograph I fondly remember is of the 1971 war hero Flying Officer Nirmaljeet Singh Sekhon, PVC, and alongside it is written, 'Who kept the faith and fought the fight; the glory theirs, the duty ours.'

'Hurry up, everyone. Line up on the veranda for the Pilot Aptitude Battery Test [PABT]; it begins at quarter to nine,' Deepa hurriedly announced as she ran from one barracks to another in her enthusiasm to discharge her duties right. She was a candidate appointed by Sqn Ldr Yadav to pass his orders to the rest of us. 'Now that's how you earn brownie points,' Aditi, an Excel academy candidate, commented plainly as she looked at the rest of us.

'Another test! They could have waited until tomorrow,' someone said.

To be able to fly the big bad machines that dominate the skies, an Indian Air Force candidate must clear the PABT. Papaji had learnt about it from one of his air force friends. But even knowing about the test didn't keep me from fretting. The test was designed to assess a candidate's aptitude to be a pilot. It wasn't just a single test but three types of tests, further subdivided into multiple tests. The Instruments Battery Test (INSB) would be a paper-pencil test, while the Sensory Motor Apparatus Test (SMA) and the Control Velocity Test (CVT) would be machine-based tests. These atrociously named tests, Papaji had told me, were necessary and quite fair on an air force's part to help select only the best pilots and prevent 'a chimp with a machine-gun' situation.

We were directed by a non-commissioned officer (NCO) (corporals and sergeants) from the veranda to a hall in a different building. Candidates were sent inside two rooms adjoining the hall. As we walked towards the room, I could hear the muffled hum of instruments, a vibration from one corner of the hall. Quietness prevailed, and we all took our respective seats. For a moment, the whole set-up felt like a secret laboratory where we were to play the part of hamsters. An officer instructor, of the rank of wing commander, briefed us on the written test.

'Good evening, candidates. You must be tired, but don't worry. We will finish this test quickly. And remember, only those who qualify in this test will appear for the machine tests. So all the best.'

I listened to him carefully. I knew I had to qualify— I had to fly, that was the aim. 'The Instruments Battery Test will comprise two parts. It is to check your ability to read and interpret the dials of an instrument panel of an aircraft . . .' he continued. The officer showed us large dummy meters—a compass meter, a climbing or diving meter, a horizon detector and an altimeter. He briefly explained their utility and functioning. 'Any questions?' he asked. No one said a word, so he called a warrant officer and a sergeant, who distributed the answer sheets. And so the test began . . .

* * *

August 1976

Very rarely does one experience joy and pain simultaneously. One must be mature enough to understand such a feeling in the first place. But I was far from mature when I first experienced this. What does a two-year-old know anyway?

I only knew that if there was something that drew my attention, I had to get to it. Curiosity ran in my veins. Little did I know that what drew my attention in the backyard of our Jhansi bungalow, one that my father had been allotted when he was posted to the Jhansi military station, would accompany me wherever I went in the future.

Betwa Nursery was in the vicinity, so Papaji and Maa had planned to start sending me there to spend time with the other kids and learn. Dada had already been going to the nursery, so I felt left behind at home. I would cry whenever Dada left for school every day. Some days I just wouldn't stop. At last, Maa reasoned with the headmistress and received permission for me to sit next to Dada in his class. But the permission was given for only two hours. Still, I was content. It was too early, Papaji's friends would say. 'But my Gunju already feels bored at home and it's hard for us to contain her energy. She needs newer things to learn,' he would tell them. A playschool was added to my daily routine as a consequence. Maa dropped me and Dada there at ten every morning and picked me up at twelve. Dada would come home later with Papaji, owing to the difference in the timings of our classes. Some days I would insist on staying at school longer. I think I liked being there. But my teacher felt otherwise.

'Come on, Gunjan . . . Come inside,' Maa called as I stopped in our garden one afternoon, listening to a strange voice that seemed to be coming from the other side of our bungalow's boundary. She had just picked me up from school and reached home.

'You want to go back to school?' she asked as she walked towards me, my little school bag still slung on her shoulder. But all my attention was focused on the sound.

'Look, I'll let you and Dada play once he's back from school. But let us first change out of this frock and eat some food, okay?' she said while caressing my face. I didn't move an inch.

'Maa . . .' I said, raising my hand to point in the direction of the sound. Gestures were an alternative to my speech, which was still developing.

'Okay, we'll play wherever you want. Now let's go inside,' she misinterpreted, as she gently picked me up and took me inside. By then the sound had stopped. As I ate my mashed potatoes and daal-rice, I kept thinking about that sound. I had heard it before.

'Wow! You ate it all, little lady. How much did you play today?' Maa commented as she fed me one last spoonful. Normally, I would make it a tough job for her. But I finished my meal quietly, since I wanted to rush outside and solve the mystery of the new sound as soon as possible. Maa sat me down on the sofa and went to the kitchen. Unattended, I leapt at the opportunity and rushed back outside, running in short baby steps straight to the backyard. Monsoon clouds had gathered in the sky and it was about to rain. There was a dump of debris at a point adjacent to the boundary wall in the backyard, which I could climb. It felt like a small hillock back then, but nevertheless, I made it to the top. For a moment I remained there, listening for that sound again, and a faint one soon reached my ears. In an attempt to catch a glimpse of what it was, I stood on my toes and leaned forward. The top of the boundary wall was rounded and for someone who had just learnt to balance herself on a flat surface, balancing here was out of the question. As a result, my attempt to sit on top of the wall failed and I fell, face down. But it was not for nothing—while still mid-air, I had caught a quick glimpse of a small brown puppy crying from under a heap of dry leaves. The mystery had been solved. The next moment, I landed on the heap of dry leaves and branches. A terrible pinching pain below my frock made me cry out loud. It was the thorns. But then, I felt something moist and wet on the side of my face. The little puppy was licking my cheek. I giggled. But then I cried again. Confused, I didn't know what to do. It was joy and pain at the same time.

The next thing I remember is the silhouette of a woman running towards me. 'Gunjan . . . Gunjan . . . Are you okay? Look, mummy is here.' It was Maa who picked me up in her arms. She had been terrified at first and had quickly scanned my body for any signs of injury. The heap of leaves had softened the impact. Rescued, I stopped crying. Relieved that I had not broken anything, Maa stopped panicking.

'It's just some scratches, Gunju. You're a strong baby, aren't you?' she said, reassuring herself more than me. She held me tightly against her chest and sighed. The puppy had hidden himself inside the heap of leaves on seeing Maa. As she got up with me in her arms and started to walk away, I started to cry again. 'Naa . . . naa,' I screamed and struggled in her arms.

'What is it, baby?' she stopped and asked. After a pause, I pointed at the heap of leaves and it was then that she saw the puppy for the first time.

'Doggy?' a confused Maa said.

I nodded. 'You came for the doggy?' she said. I nodded again. For a moment she looked at the puppy, and then at me. 'Umm . . . his mama will come and take him. Let's go now.' No sooner had she said this than I launched into incessant sobs. 'Hey! Ssshhh. *Beta*, what happened?' She began to wipe my tears. The puppy, too, let out squeals in unison. I raised my hand towards the sky and she could see that I was pointing at the dark clouds. 'Oh, Gunjan!' she said as she realized what I meant. 'You don't want the doggy to get wet! Okay, let's take him inside. Will you stop crying then?' Slowly, I calmed down. Maa gently placed me on the ground and reached for the puppy, who at first scrambled deeper inside the leaves, but Maa picked it up in her right hand. I clapped and giggled as she smiled at me. A drop of rain fell on my cheek where the trail of tears had just dried. The puppy's large eyes were fixed on me. I held Maa's left hand and, together, the three of us marched back inside our house.

It rained cats and dogs that afternoon. Inside, Maa bathed me and my new friend, dried us both and sat us on the veranda when Papaji's Gypsy arrived. Papaji held Dada close and rushed inside as his driver followed him, holding an umbrella that hardly saved them from the incessant rain. 'A puppy!' Dada exclaimed happily on seeing the pup sitting next to me, freed himself from Papaji's arm and ran towards us. 'Can we keep him? Are we keeping him?' he asked.

'Where did he come from?' a surprised Papaji asked Maa. 'Your daughter rescued this one,' Maa said. 'Go change first, I'll tell you about it over lunch.' Papaji gazed at me, smiled and nodded. Meanwhile, Dada petted the puppy with his wet hands.

Papaji was able to convince Maa and they mutually agreed to let the pup stay. Chimpu became an inseparable member of the family in no time. Dada named the puppy after one of the characters in Grandmother's bedtime stories. For a few days I resisted going to the playschool in the morning, and spent the entire time with Chimpu. Papaji got him vaccinated and brought home dog food. Maa made sure of the hygiene in and around the house— 'Chimpu will not sleep in your bed' and 'Chimpu will not eat from your hands'. She set ground rules in the house only to see them broken every day. Chimpu's brown hair could be found everywhere—on the sofa, on the carpet, on the veranda, in the bathroom, on our beds and on our clothes. He even went on the occasional picnic with us. Papaji would put him in his scooter's front basket during the journey. I was happy. I made a lot of memories with Chimpu. Happy memories.

One afternoon in September, Maa was taking a nap, while Chimpu, Dada and I played on the veranda under Papaji's supervision. Dada and I chased Chimpu, who manoeuvred quicker than the two of us. In a daring attempt to catch Chimpu, Dada took a miscalculated dive and ended up almost crushing Chimpu, who then let out two or three feeble cries and ran inside on three legs instead of four. 'Dada . . . Timpu . . . no,' was all I could manage to say to Dada. I understood that he had hurt Chimpu. Dada pulled up his knickers and gestured with a finger on his lips, hoping I would stay quiet. He tiptoed to take a look at Papaji and saw him dozing in the chair, a book in his hand. Dada then tilted his head and gestured for me to follow him inside the house. I trod softly behind him in my flowery pyjamas. We saw Chimpu lying on his mattress, licking his front right paw, the one that was hurt. On seeing this, I curled up my lower lip and frowned at Dada. 'Sorry Gunju, I didn't mean it,' Dada said. 'Let's make his pain go away. Okay?' I understood him and nodded. He then cupped his chin and began to think. I imitated him and cupped my chin too. A scared Chimpu looked at us as we devised another devilry.

For a while we stood there, doing nothing. Then I saw something that reminded me of Papaji's remedy. Two nights ago, Maa had twisted her ankle at Colonel Usha's place after dinner. Upon reaching home, I had seen Papaji massage Maa's ankle with something in a red glass bottle. I could see that bottle on the kitchen shelf. I tugged at Dada's arm and pulled him inside the kitchen. 'What is it?' he asked. I pointed towards the bottle and said, 'Dada . . . botil . . . Chimpu pain go.' He, too, understood what I meant, and since he was taller than me, had to go get the bottle. Somehow, he managed. The bottle was uncorked and a hand towel was made to soak in most of its contents. I covered my nose with one hand—the smell was sharp, pungent. I ran to Chimpu with the towel and started to wipe his right paw with it. Unsure, Dada watched me doing it. Chimpu's fur was soaked in the liquid from the towel and he started to lick it. After a while, Chimpu got up— on all fours. I smiled, thinking my remedy had worked.

Chimpu snatched the towel from my hand and began to lick it too. I looked at Dada with a smile of victory.

A confused Dada stared at Chimpu, who kept licking the towel for the next few minutes until his hind legs dwindled a little and he fell sideways. However, he managed to get up and dash outside, zigzagging, trying hard to keep his balance. The puppy paused mid-stride on the veranda and started to bark and howl weirdly at Papaji, waking him from his slumber. Chimpu took a few steps towards him, growling his puppy growl, and fell, off-balance. Papaji helped a struggling Chimpu up. As soon as Chimpu was up again, he turned back and ran inside, swaying left and right. Papaji followed him. We stood near the kitchen as Chimpu ran past us, and, like an unguided missile, banged his head into the base of a long, thin flower vase. Before Papaji could reach for it, the vase hit the floor and shattered into pieces. 'Oh no!' Papaji muttered.

'What happened?' It was Maa's voice from inside the bedroom. She came out at once and stared at the scattered pieces of her favourite flower vase, surprised. A questioning stare swept from Papaji to the two of us. She carefully made her way through the broken pieces and found Chimpu lying with all fours up in the air near the broken base of the vase, all four paws in the air, continuously in motion, as if running. Papaji bent forward and lifted Chimpu in his arms, raised him closer to his face and sniffed. Chimpu was now almost unconscious. The twitching of Papaji's facial muscles signalled that something was wrong. Maa found the hand towel and the opened bottle, the evidence of something that now appeared to be a crime. Dada and I stood silent, trying to appear innocent. 'What did you two do?' Maa asked Dada very calmly. At first, Dada didn't say a word, terrified from the moment the vase had broken. But then Maa consoled him, 'It's okay, beta, don't worry about the vase. I just want to know what happened. Or Chimpu will be hurt. You do not want that to happen, right?' Slowly, Dada told them about the whole incident.

'So you're saying it was Gunju's idea?' Maa said as Dada nodded. She then looked at Papaji, who was smiling. 'She used your rum-massage formula! She's your typical *fauji* kid,' Maa concluded, and then, after a moment of pause, both of them burst into uncontrollable laughter. 'We have to teach our curious kid that rum is not the solution to all problems,' Papaji said as he laughed. Dada and I kept looking at each other, still. Chimpu barked twice and fell unconscious again, only to wake up after five long hours of deep slumber.

* * *

As a child, I was secure within my family. The challenge for my parents was to create a learning environment that was both safe, and novel and stimulating—and they undoubtedly succeeded at it. Sometimes, a child's ways of exploration can be dangerous. The same could have happened with me. I had seen my parents put metal objects into electric sockets, fiddle with radio parts, use a matchstick to start a fire and push buttons on electronic devices. I was a great mimic, so my curiosity would often send me out to explore. I might have put a fork in the electric socket, I might have taken things apart, I might have ended up harming myself. But my parents ensured that they were always vigilant, supervising my explorations and fostering in me a sense of freedom. Therefore, my curiosity was channelled well and it turned me into a quick learner.

The INSB test was a cakewalk. Although that wasn't the case with many others. Hema was a bit disappointed— she was confused during the test and might have written the answers wrong. But I was relieved that it was over. The officer instructor collected the answer sheets and called out our names, two candidates at a time, sending us in pairs to adjacent rooms, where the instrumental humming of machines had been coming from. I was both curious and nervous at the same time. When I walked through the door into the first room, I saw two machines with joysticks, buttons and screens. *Would I be able to understand it?* But many before me had made sense of it and passed; it shouldn't be a problem, I told myself. There was an instructor sergeant inside who began his briefing, 'Good evening to you both, welcome to the Sensory Motor Apparatus Test. It may sound complex, but it is a simple test . . .'

The test was just like playing a console game, but aimed at measuring the psychomotor coordination skills of the candidate. There were two rectangles on a black screen—a small rectangle inside a bigger one. There was a dot on the screen, which had to be adjusted inside the small rectangle with a joystick. Using one's peripheral vision, one had to press the buttons on an adjacent panel as they lit up. A red and green light on the screen had to be switched off using one's left hand. All this had to be done quickly and simultaneously. The second test was the Control Velocity Test. A small magnetic dot had to be superimposed on holes, which ran in two horizontal lines on a rotating drum, using a joystick.

After the briefing was over, the sergeant asked us if we were ready. I placed my hand on my chest number. I was reminded of Papaji's words, 'Four is your lucky number, Gunjan.' He would often tell me when I was younger that he believed in numerology. The words had stuck, for some reason. I took a deep breath, held the joystick firmly, stared at the screen, narrowed my eyes and replied to the instructor, 'I'm ready.'

FOUR

Wars are not won by tanks, ships, guns, fighter jets, submarines or nuclear bombs—wars are won by human beings. The world's greatest armies fighting in the greatest wars understood that war was a business, and if one was to win at it, one would have to conduct it according to established principles. How does one find a workforce fit enough to fight in a war? Eventually, men and women, whose trade it was to find a solution to problems such as these were consulted—psychologists who devised tests, by means of which they were able to measure intelligence, aptitude and adaptability. These tests helped handpick men and women fit to become future leaders, and also helped weed out the incompetent. Ingenious schemes were put into operation to bring together a group of individuals of similar intellectual standard to facilitate military training. It all went well for the psychologists. As a result, it was concluded that the only thing that mattered in war, besides physical strength, was mental attitude. Only the greatest leaders in history have been able to understand and exploit it.

For any leader, defeat is just an attitude; it resides in the mind and is not a physical condition. And this attitude varies from person to person. To find a person in possession of the right kind of mental attitude and psychological strength required to lead in battle, the Indian defence forces came up with a sequence of psychological tests that formed the major chunk of the SSB exam: the Word Association Test (WAT), the Thematic Appreciation Test (TAT), the Self-Description (SD) test and the Situation Reaction Test (SRT). These might just sound like acronyms to many, but for defence aspirants, these are the devils that stand at the gates of any SSB centre, ready to peek into the darkest corners of their minds and reveal their true, hidden selves. The tests are written against the constraints of time as a requirement. Hence, the candidate is unable to hide his/her true feelings, and the psychologist is able to read the actual personality of the candidate while he/she gives his/her responses in terms of thoughts, feelings and actions. As psychologists claim, no amount of coaching can help a candidate skirt around these psychological tests. Those who have tried have ended up being rejected in the end. The rate of error has to be zero—one wrong selection and an entire platoon, battalion or even a division may suffer. Someone can be denied for being too young, too old, for having flat feet, anxiety, phobias and so on. Someone can be denied for not being physically fit, for not running a required course in time or for not doing the required number of push-ups. Similarly, someone whose mental attitude doesn't match the required standards can also be denied. Psychological tests help in this process of filtration.

Inevitably, I appeared for these psychological tests on our second day of the SSB interview. Weariness still lay heavy on me from the night before. I remember dreaming about sitting in front of the machines with joysticks and screens; the PABT had taken quite a toll on me. Deepa was given orders for the day, which she passed on to all of us after she woke us early on the second day. 'How dutiful!' Aditi commented wryly as soon as Deepa had left the room.

'Why, are you jealous?' Hema just couldn't contain herself.

'What's your problem?' Aditi retorted.

'How about you being nice for once? It might come in handy for you,' Hema replied. Aditi ignored her and walked out of the barracks.

'Let it be,' I nudged Hema. 'We don't want our day to start with unnecessary arguments, do we?'

'Did you see her yesterday, in front of the instructors? As if she was the most social and friendly human being here among us!' Hema said as she ironed her shirt. 'Well, she won't be able to pretend today. Psychological tests are no joke.'

'Umm . . . any advice for me?' I asked her as I looked at myself in the mirror. The dress for the day was dark pants with a plain shirt and brogues, as per our instructions. I had tied my hair into a bun, as had already been agreed upon between Hema and me after a half-hour discussion the night before. 'You'll do just fine, *nannageleya.** Just make sure you attempt all the questions and that your answers convey positivity,' she said as she tied her hair.

'Well . . . I'll remember.' I said.

After the 'fall-in' and count-up, and a quick briefing outside the examination hall by Sqn Ldr Yadav, we were seated inside. A digital stopwatch was hung on the front wall and it read '0630h'. A projector cast a blank display on a huge whiteboard in front of the wall. Answer sheets were distributed to all. A fan running in one corner made a creaking sound. Other than that, there was absolute silence. 'So candidates, all set?' Sqn Ldr Yadav asked. Everyone

---

* Nannageleya means 'my friend' in Kannada.

replied with a 'yes sir' in unison. The first test began after the projector flashed, and a countdown from ten ended.

The TAT entailed writing twelve stories about the pictures that were shown to us one after the other on the screen. We were given thirty seconds to glance at a picture and four minutes to write the story, after which the next picture would flash. The twelfth one was a blank screen. Papaji had already spoken to me about this. I was to link this twelfth story to a momentous reflection on my life. *You may not be able to write more than eight to ten lines in the stipulated four minutes. As a rough yardstick, write about two lines for what could have led to this scene, four lines on what you perceive is presently going on in the scene and about four more lines to describe what the logical outcome of the scene could be, according to you,* Papaji had told me. *The views conveyed by you in the story will reflect your social attitude and depict the responsibilities you feel towards others in the society. Do not unnecessarily perceive a problem when it is not shown in the picture—that signals a pessimistic bent of mind. Do not write a wishful story, Gunju, and whatever you write, lead it towards some conclusion.*

I remember sticking to these guidelines when I attempted the test. After it was over, the fingers on my right hand hurt from all the writing I had done at breakneck speed.

It was like a marathon of tests that day. The WAT started right after the answer sheets for the TAT were collected.

The lesser the time, the lower the chances for someone to outsmart the tests. I didn't even get time to drink water from the glass kept on my desk. Sixty words were flashed on the screen, each for a duration of fifteen seconds. We were required to write the first thoughts that came to our minds on seeing each word. *Do not mistake this test for a sentence-making exercise. Do not falter in the very approach to this particular test,* Papaji had strictly advised me. Of the sixty words, some words were related to intellectual quotient, some to social attributes, some were meant to reflect effectiveness as part of a team, while some were aimed at depicting a candidate's dynamism. Responses to these words would be analysed by psychologists. These responses, including the responses of the previous test, would help draw a final descriptive personality of each candidate. To attempt this test and follow Papaji's guidelines at the same time in only fifteen seconds per word seemed rather difficult. Somehow, I managed to attempt fifty-three words in the given time. Not bad! Hema could attempt only forty, she would tell me later.

Right after the WAT, we had to take the SRT. Hardly a moment of respite was allowed. I cracked my knuckles and neck, preparing myself for what was coming next. The SRT is aimed at analysing a candidate's spontaneous and instinctive responses to unfamiliar, stressful and life-like situations. Booklets containing incomplete statements were distributed to us, a total of sixty situations for candidates to complete. We were given thirty minutes, and precisely thirty seconds each to complete a single situation. The rules were simple, Papaji had told me. *A response to a situation/statement should be given in a methodical manner, which is brief but complete in all its aspects; for example, if you see a fire incident, you must start by calling the fire brigade, followed by gathering people nearby and organizing them into parties, such as the rescue and fire-extinguishing parties, some to arrange for transport to take the injured to the hospital, then others to inform police authorities and lastly, to inform the next of kin of the injured person. Illogical bravado must always be avoided. As an example, fighting alone with a number of hoodlums on seeing them teasing a girl, or jumping into a river to save someone when the situation states that you are a non-swimmer will get you nothing but a negative assessment. One must remain realistic and take only calculated risks when writing one's responses. But empathy and moral responsibility towards society should be kept in mind.*

All I remember was that I focused on organizing my thoughts while writing my responses and made sure to keep the basics in mind. I ended up writing fifty-five responses before Sqn Ldr Yadav asked us to put our pens down. I looked around to see most faces disappointed. But I was fairly content with my performance, though I didn't know how it would be judged. Next was the SD. We were required to write on a blank sheet of paper what we felt our family members, friends and teachers thought about us. Both the positive aspects of our personality and the areas we felt needed improvement were required to be mentioned. By the time the digital clock read '0900h', the tests were done.

'*O devare*, I've never written so many stories ever in my life before,' Hema said as we walked out of the examination hall. 'I can be a novelist now.'

'Yes, but please don't write anything on psychology. I've had my share of it in just a day,' I said, and we laughed.

'Everyone, proceed for breakfast, please,' Deepa announced to the scattered groups of girls. We headed for the mess. It was the day I learnt how hungry mental exhaustion could make you feel. I'd never really worried much about exams and tests back in school or college, but this wasn't just an exam or a test. My dreams, and Papaji's, were at stake.

'Why is everyone reading and mugging up?' I asked Hema at the breakfast table. There was silence inside the mess and most of the tables had more notes laid out than plates. Almost every girl had her face buried in the pages of either handwritten notes or textbooks. And there I was, deciding whether to eat my toast with butter or with fruit jam. 'I don't know,' Hema said, equally clueless.

'Preparing for the group discussion,' chipped in Prabhdeep, one of our fellow candidates sitting in front of us. 'We're brushing up on our GK and current affairs.'

'So we go for the GD after the breakfast?' I asked.

Prabhdeep nodded. 'Here, take a look if you want to.' She offered her current affairs notes to me. Reluctantly, I took them.

I wasn't really sure I'd even give them a read. General knowledge was a grey area and the notes only scared me more. Hema could see the discomfort I felt when talking about it.

'Well, it isn't necessary to be Derek O'Brien when you appear for the GD,' Hema said as she took the notes from me and gave them back to Prabhdeep.

'Thanks anyway, Prabhdeep,' I said with a forced smile. Prabhdeep smiled back and continued to read her notes. The thought of appearing for the GD without any preparation vanquished my hunger. I put the toast back on my plate and walked out of the mess.

'Wait for me,' Hema followed me to the veranda outside in a run, caught her breath and continued, 'we don't have to worry about the GD. We'll do just fine.' I turned to face her and smiled.

'I don't even read the newspaper. I just don't know what's happening in the world. Bollywood, yes, that's something you can ask me about,' I said as we strolled, trying to de-stress together.

'Who reads newspapers? Ugh . . . there are better things to do. And about the GD, we'll cross that bridge when we get to it,' Hema said as we circled the veranda. We chatted for a while until we were made to assemble for the exam near the football field.

It was half past ten on a sunny morning. The seating was arranged in groups of twelve chairs placed in a semicircle in front of the instructors' tables inside a vast training shed. A pair of ropes hung from pillars in one corner of the shed and a gymnast's horse rested in another. A few dumb-bells were stacked neatly near the ropes. Physical training facilities could be found in every defence establishment. Nine groups had been formed, with roughly twelve candidates in each group. Unfortunately, or otherwise, three of those four candidates from the Excel institute, those who had cleared the screening, had ended up in my group. Aditi, too, was among them. As we took our seats, Aditi winked at the other two and I understood that they were up to something. An officer instructor came to each group and disclosed the topic of the group discussion. 'Good morning, candidates, I'm Sqn Ldr A.S. Virk. I'll be conducting this group discussion. Let us get over with the introductions quickly.' He was a well-built, smart-looking turbaned officer dressed in a mufti. 'A few ground rules before we begin. During the conduct of this entire GD, keep in mind that it's a discussion and not a debate. You will be given two minutes to think about the topic and you're not allowed to talk to each other while you do so.

Let's make it an intellectually stimulating session.' Even as I listened, I could not help but think about what the topic would be. And then the bomb was dropped. 'Your topic is: Who should control the distribution of the Kaveri river water—the Central government or the states? Your preparation time starts as soon as I ring the bell, and when I ring it again, please begin the discussion.'

I could feel patches of sweat form on the back of my shirt as the seconds passed. I wiped the beads of sweat from my forehead. My knowledge of this topic was as good as nothing. I just sat there, counting the seconds, nervous as I was. A lot of thoughts streamed into my mind in those two minutes. *How can you let one GD decide the outcome of your SSB interview? Do something, Gunjan Saxena, there has to be a way.* No sooner had the bell rung than the Excel girls leapt into the discussion, seizing the initiative. All hell broke loose! Loud voices rang in my ears as I sat there, silent. 'Fish market' is the term that I would use to describe the scene. Even as everyone shouted in desperation to make the instructor hear what they had to say, I closed my eyes for a moment—a memory flashed before my eyes and left me with the solution that would eventually help get me through this test.

FIVE

December 1978

'Okay, that's enough. Get out of there now, or Babaji will scold you,' Maa chided Dada and me as we played in the ankle-length water at the entrance of the Golden Temple in Amritsar. A turbaned saint, dressed in dark-blue overalls, stared at us with a smile behind his thick beard. He stood at attention, guarding the entrance with a traditional spear in his hand. It didn't matter to us if the water was freezing cold. We were enjoying ourselves. It was a bright sunny Sunday in the peak of winter and Papaji had planned to take us out. He had been posted to Amritsar recently. The Golden Temple was not very far from the cantonment, and all four of us loved going there. Where Maa and Papaji found peace in the serenity of the soothing Gurbani that echoed on the premises, Dada and I loved to play in its vast marble corridors and enjoyed feeding 'kadah prasad' to the fish in the holy pond. Although Papaji was an atheist, something about the Golden Temple drew him to it.

'Only if you promise to take us for langar,' I had negotiated with Maa and she had nodded in approval. Dada and I trotted carelessly ahead of Maa and Papaji, barefoot on the cold marble. 'Keep your heads covered with the rumala, both of you,' Maa's instruction followed us as we made for the stairs. From the arched entrance, the first thing that came into view was the shining spectacle of Darbar Sahib covered in gold. A reflection of its gilt-edged temple shimmered in the water of the holy pool that surrounded it. The surrealism of the view mesmerized me like always and I stood at the edge of the staircase, folding my hands in veneration, imitating Dada. Verses of Gurbani rang out in a comforting tune.

'Why are there four entrances, Maa?' I asked as we began our parikrama around the temple.

'It is because the temple is open from the four cardinal directions, so people can enter from any side, symbolizing openness towards all types of people,' Maa told me. 'Every person is equal, Gunjan beta, so everyone must have equal rights and privileges.' I returned a rather confused look. 'If I give a chocolate to Dada and not to you, would you like it?' she tried to simplify it. I shook my head. 'That is why we should treat everyone equally.'

We entered the langar hall, the community kitchen, and sat in line on the floor with all the other visitors. 'You see this? Everyone sits on the same floor and eats the same food. Regardless of whether you are a king or a beggar, you are treated alike here,' Maa continued our conversation from before.

'I understand, Maa,' I replied.

A volunteer poured daal on to our steel plates, another gave us chapatis, yoghurt and kheer. Simple but delicious. Papaji loved the kheer, and I enjoyed the daal.

We walked towards the temple after the langar. As we entered the queue of the main darbar, the hall, I saw a Sikh saint standing behind a huge bronze platter full of kadah prasad, asking visitors for their leaf bowls. I narrowed my eyes to see that he poured all of the kadah prasad from their leaf bowls into the platter and returned half of it in the same leaf bowl. 'Why does he take prasad from everyone, Maa?' reluctant to let him have our leaf bowl, I asked her.

'So that everyone's offerings are mixed together and everyone gets an equal share from the common platter. Remember what I told you—everyone must be treated equally,' Maa replied.

Even though I understood what she said, I kept a strict watch on the saint as he took the kadah prasad from our bowl. It was so delicious that I didn't want him to keep any of it. But I guess my frown only made him smile more.

Such visits were some of the earliest memories I could remember. Maa and Papaji made the best use of every opportunity to teach us the values that they considered necessary. I had also started to enjoy our stay in Amritsar. With so many places to travel to, so much variety in food to choose from, and the sheer fun-loving spirit and bonhomie among the people, Amritsar became part of me even before I could realize it. No wonder it is called 'Sifti da ghar', or the adorable abode. Another memory from Amritsar that was very dear to me was of Tiny Tots School. Dada and I were admitted to the school soon after the winter season, in the beginning of 1979. Two reasons why our parents chose the school, besides its soaring reputation, were that it was in the vicinity of the cantonment and a school-bus service was available. Dada liked the school for its large playground, whereas I liked it for its bright uniform—a dark-blue T-shirt and red shorts. Rita Ma'am, the principal, even let the girls wear colourful ribbons in their plaits. And there was a flower bed on the school's front veranda, which I loved the most. I'd pluck a flower every day to give to Ms Srishti, my favourite teacher, whom I used to affectionately call 'Titli Ma'am'. She'd give me candy in return.

'Dada, get up, or we'll miss the bus,' I would sit on top of Dada and try to wake him up; and he would pull the quilt to his face again. 'Two more minutes,' Dada would murmur, half asleep. It had been two months since we had joined Tiny Tots. I would usually get up on my own, but waking Dada up on time was no easy task.

'Wake up, both of you,' Maa would enter the room with two glasses of warm choco-malt milk. Behind her trailed Chimpu, ready to jump on Dada and lick his face. Every day, Papaji would go for his morning PT while Maa would get us ready for school. She would tie my hair into plaits as I drank my glass of milk. Sometimes I'd get jealous of Dada's low-maintenance crew-cut hairstyle. Sanjay Bhaiya, Papaji's *sahayak*, or aide, helped Maa pack our breakfast every morning. Dada and I never took the same food for our tiffins. Our demands always differed, and Maa never denied cooking separately for us. For the rest of the meals, there was a simple rule of acceptance, applicable to all members of the Saxena family. As always, Maa dropped us till the bus stop, which was just a minute away from home. As always, she made us carry our school bags and water bottles ourselves. As always, we kissed her goodbye and got into the bright yellow minibus from Tiny Tots when it arrived.

'He's on my seat, Dada,' I whispered on seeing a boy occupying my usual spot as we walked towards the back.

Dada walked up to him and his intimidating stare was enough to get the seat vacated. My elder brother was also my unpaid personal bodyguard. Besides, Papaji's instructions included that he look out for me during school hours. The little devil that I was, I made full use of it. 'Next time, you better talk to people yourself,' Dada said as he helped me sit. 'Anyway, you remember what I told you yesterday, right?'

'Yes! I remember.' Like a dutiful sister, I punctuated my words with a nod.

'Good girl!' Dada said.

'Will you let me play with your friends then?' I tried to get reassurance for the terms from a day before. Dada's friends were the only friends I had. They would be my only friends for a long time to come.

'I will. I promise,' Dada said and extended his pinkie finger. I extended mine to lock it with his, and for the umpteenth time since the previous day, we bound ourselves into this agreement.

Dada had tasked me with a job I considered very important, so much so that I even forgot to pluck a flower for Titli Ma'am that day—all my focus was on the task at hand. Even though I didn't know how to read time on the clock, I knew when the bell for recess rang, since I remembered the position of the clock's arms. I kept staring at the wall clock through all the periods. As the clock's arms inched closer to the position, I took out my tiffin and readied myself for a sprint. The bell rang. The joy of recess converted into a collective cheer, which echoed from all directions. I got out of my seat and ran as fast as I could. Little but quick steps, and careful manoeuvring through the crowd of students streaming into the corridor took me out of the classroom building to the playground. I locked my sights on my target. I made a run for it. There was nobody to contest it when I reached and occupied my seat on the tyre swing. It took me a while to catch my breath. But I was happy. *Dada would be so proud*. Ten minutes later, another bell rang. Recess for the students in the first grade had commenced. For Upper KG and below, recess started much earlier. That is why Dada had charged me with the task of keeping the tyre swing occupied till he came around. That swing was a favourite with all the senior boys. Many came running towards it, returning disappointed on hearing me say, 'It's for my Dada; you go away.' Finally, Dada let me play with his friends when he came to see that I'd done the task he had asked me to do.

I continued this for a couple of days. Together, Dada and I had devised a plan that suited both of us. He got the tyre swing and I got his friends. This, however, didn't sit well with some of the boys. Hostility brewed among the senior-most of them. Mutiny was imminent. 'Gunjan from KG' became a notorious figure on the playground premises. Consequently, things took a bad turn one day.

'Give me the tyre,' a burly sardar boy of the second standard stood in front of me as I sat on the tyre swing that day. 'No,' I replied grimly, 'I'll only give it to Dada.'

'Give it to me or I'll teach you and your Dada a lesson today,' he took a step forward, with hands on his waist as he warned me. A frown appeared on his round face. His red *patka* screened the sun and his shadow fell on me. Terrified but resolute, I replied, 'I will not give it to you.' From the corner of my eyes I saw two other boys join him to his left and right. Scared, I buried my neck in my sweater.

'I'm asking you one last time,' he said.

I desperately hoped for Dada to show up. But I was not going to give up. 'Only my Dada will get the swing.' Even as I said this, I tightened my grip on the ropes of the swing. The sardar boy came closer and tugged at my arm. The tiffin fell from my lap and on to the ground, its contents scattered about it. There was no sign of Dada. 'No. No!' I struggled to keep my grip. The other two boys came forward to help the sardar boy. But muscle finally won against might. The three of them held me back, both my arms in their tight grip and pushed me so hard that I fell to the ground, and took two rolls before I stopped. I felt a sharp pain in my right knee. Slowly, I got up, sat on the ground and hugged my knees against my chest. Blood oozed from the gash in my fingers as I held on to the scraped knee. The three boys let out a victorious laugh. I broke into loud sobs. There was still no sign of Dada.

Maa received a call from my teacher and came to school to pick me up. I was taken to the first aid room, where they dressed my wound. I'd told them all I had tripped and fallen. Dada would get a good scolding if I'd told them the truth. Maa took me home. I wasn't crying any more. I was simply angry. Very angry.

'Where were you?' I asked Dada heatedly after he came home. Maa was in the kitchen. I was resting my leg on the sofa. Dada learnt about the entire incident from the other children in the school bus.

'We were punished by Ms Geeta for not finishing our homework. She made us stand facing the wall for half of the recess,' Dada said as he examined the dressing on my leg. He knew the wound was bad. It made him angry too.

'Why did you not give them the swing? Why are you so stupid?' he said.

'Why are you shouting at me? I didn't know you were not going to come,' I replied.

'How could you let yourself get hurt because of a swing, stupid?' Dada's concern frustrated him, and he stomped out of the living room.

As he left, Papaji entered. On seeing the dressing on my knee, he at once hung his beret on the stand and walked towards me. 'What happened to my little girl?' he crooned.

I hugged him and started to cry. 'It's okay. It's just a scratch. You're stronger than this,' Papaji hugged me back. Maa had told Papaji everything on the telephone. For a while, I stayed in Papaji's arms. He carefully lifted me and carried me to my room when he realized that I had fallen asleep. He was there in the evening when I woke up, dozing by my side. Chimpu was asleep on his lap. As I struggled to get up, I felt an unbearable pain shoot up my knee when I tried to fold my leg. 'Don't move the leg, beta,' Papaji woke up and said. He helped me sit. 'Now tell me, how did this happen?' he asked as he stroked my head. 'I tripped and fell.' Knowing I was lying to him, I averted my eyes.

'That story is for others, not me. So, tell me what happened, Gunju. It's okay,' he asked again. I looked into his eyes and narrated everything that had happened. 'Dada knows too. He will take care of that boy,' I concluded.

Papaji took a deep breath, held my hand in his and said, 'It is not Dada's fight. It is your fight, Gunju.'

I looked at him with confusion on my face. 'Look, what happened to you was bad, right?' he asked, and I nodded. 'Was it unjust?' he asked. I nodded as I listened to him. 'Was Dada there to protect you?' he asked.

'No,' I replied, unhappily.

'When you grow up to be a big girl, there will be many more fights. Anshu loves you a lot, but he might not always be there to protect you,' he said.

'But where will Dada go?' I threw an innocent question at him.

'Well, let's just say, Anshu goes to college or gets a job in a different city. What then?' Papaji asked, to which I had no answer. I dropped my shoulders and looked down. 'Learn to fight your own fights, Gunju,' Papaji gently lifted my chin with his finger. 'Make yourself so strong that nobody picks a fight with you. They just won't if they know that this girl will fight back,' Papaji spoke softly, yet firmly. I listened.

'But those boys were big boys,' I said.

'No matter how big your problem is, you should face it. If you cannot face it with strength, then apply your mind,' Papaji pressed his index finger to my forehead. 'The mind always wins over muscle. Now when you go to school after your knee gets better, *make yourself heard*. Let them know they cannot mess with my little girl. Finish every fight anyone picks with you. All you need to do is devise a strategy.' He then looked at my knee and continued, 'People get hurt in a fight. You might get hurt many times. But each wound will make you stronger. Do you get it?'

Even though it took me a while to understand what he meant, I nodded and raised my arms to hug him. He hugged me back. 'Don't fight back with an intention to hurt someone—fight back only to make sure they hear you . . .'

I spent the next week in bed, until my wound had healed enough for me to be able to walk. The only thing I had liked about the entire week was that I was being given full attention. All my demands were being met; there was no restriction on chocolates or chowmein. And there was no homework. But all this while I had been thinking about the things Papaji had told me. All this while, I had been devising a strategy. After a week, I went to school again. I forgot to pluck a flower for Titli Ma'am again. My mind was elsewhere. I waited through all the periods for the clock's arms to strike recess. And as the bell rang, I ran towards the playground, limping. The ropes of the tyre swing were tied to an iron bar that rested on two iron poles on either side. There was a similar frame behind it, but without any swing on it. I took out a small ball of wool from my pocket, one I had slipped into my bag from Maa's craft material that morning. I tied one end of the string to the right pole, stretched it taut and tied the other end to the left pole. Just beyond the string, I made a small puddle of water using my water bottle and poured into it the contents of an entire bottle of ink I'd stolen from Maa's collection as well. Below the tyre swing, on the ground, I kept something that could lure every boy in school—marbles. After one final check, I hid myself behind a nearby guava tree. I felt a fire in my belly as I waited. The sardar boy and his two friends had started occupying the tyre swing every day, a girl in my class had told me. So I knew they would come. When they came, they saw the sparkling round marbles and bent to pick them up. That was when I took position behind them.

'Don't you ever push me again!' I shouted at the top of my voice, as I stood, holding the ropes of the tyre swing that I had pulled towards me. Startled, the three of them turned to look at me. With all the force I had, I swung the tyre towards them. It pushed the three of them back, and as they toppled backwards, they tripped on the string of wool and fell down. Splashes of muddy water splattered in all directions as they landed in the puddle I had made earlier. The more they tried to get up, the more they slipped and fell into it. In front of the swinging tyre, I stood with my hands resting on my waist as I saw them struggle, but only getting more dirty and stained. After standing there for one more moment, I ran back inside.

Of course, there were consequences. Maa and Papaji were called in by the principal. Maa was astonished to learn about what I had done and how I had done it. She and the principal kept discussing the treatment for my behaviour while I sat in one corner, looking at Papaji, who looked back at me. And then, he smiled. I smiled back.

* * *

During the discussion, the Excel girls spoke so loudly that the other girls could hardly be heard over them. Almost half a minute had passed, and I was still thinking about whether I would be able to make it through the GD. *Make yourself heard,* Papaji's words echoed in my mind. *All you need to do is to devise a strategy.* Without wasting any time, I started working on my strategy. *Don't worry, there are still five minutes left,* I said to myself. My plan was simple, but I didn't know if it would work. I listened to all the girls speak about the topic and recorded the facts that were given by them. Basically, I took the information from their arguments and educated myself right there.

'Tamil Nadu has almost 54 per cent of the basin area. Thousands of square kilometres of agricultural land are dependent on this river's water. The state of Tamil Nadu should maintain the flow,' Chest Number 16 said.

'But the river originates in Karnataka. I believe Karnataka should be given primary control,' Chest Number 25 said.

'I agree with Chest Number 25,' two other girls said.

'Mysore was the first to be allowed to construct a dam, and Madras had agreed to it in 1924. So Karnataka has the oldest right to maintain the flow of the Kaveri's waters,' Chest Number 68 said.

'But it was Tamil Nadu that first proposed the constitution of the Cauvery Tribunal, in 1986. The tribunal was formed in 1990, after so much effort put in by the state. All that hard work cannot go in vain,' said Chest Number 16.

'Kaveri is the lifeblood of both, Karnataka and Tamil Nadu. I think the governments of both the states should be allowed an equal part in its share and control,' Chest Number 99 said.

'But Karnataka has ceased supply of water to Tamil Nadu,' Chest Number 68 said.

The discussion, which had turned into a debate, went on for another two minutes as I listened. But time pressed on and I realized that if I didn't speak now, I would have to pay for it heavily. Not knowing which state to side with, I made an entirely different point when I barged in and said, 'Why should any state be given control of a resource that belongs to the country?' To my surprise, all the candidates went silent for a split second and before anyone could start again, I continued, 'It should be a nation's responsibility to take care of its waters. Every state government will think of its own benefit, and we have been witnessing this since

Independence. That is why Karnataka rejected the tribunal award in 1991. And Tamil Nadu has been resisting the building of dams by Karnataka while it continues to build its own. The Kaveri is not a state's property—it is a nation's resource.'

'But the Central government, too, has never provided a reasonable solution,' Chest Number 68 countered.

'You may be right,' I said, and continued, 'the Central government alone cannot find a solution. We, as a nation, have to come together on this matter. Agencies, like power corporations and even small-scale industries that use its water, should be made accountable and responsible for its maintenance. The flow of water should depend on the quarterly results of this upkeep and careful calculation of a state's predicted requirements. Everyone who uses the Kaveri's waters must be bound to a uniform code to avoid exploitation of the river, and to minimize water pollution. After all, who must rightly control the river-water flow isn't the question—rather, we must think about how to do it effectively, to suit everyone's interests, while avoiding exploitation and unfair conduct. This is what the Central and the state governments should decide upon. The Centre alone, or the states alone, cannot solve this problem. But a nation can.'

There was a brief pause in my argument as I stopped to catch my breath. Then the discussion resumed, but I didn't speak any further until the bell rang, indicating that the time was up. Sqn Ldr Virk asked us to remain silent as he scribbled something on a piece of paper. 'All right, girls, all of you spoke well. There's no marking scheme, so I can't tell you how much each of you has scored. I guess the final results will tell you that,' the officer said as he got up with his file. As he left, he looked at me, smiled and said, 'Chest Number 4, you united a divided conversation. Keep it up.'

'Thank you, Sir,' I said and looked at the girls sitting next to me from the corner of my eyes. They whispered something to each other.

As soon as the group dispersed, I hurried towards the PCO booth next to the cafeteria and called up Papaji. 'You once told me to make myself heard when it was required,' I said to him.

'Yes, I remember. What about it?' he asked, to which I replied with a content smile, 'Today, they heard me.'

SIX

'Sometimes I wish I too had a palace,' Hema sighed. We were standing outside the Mysore Palace, which was lit up by hundreds of lights. 'A king-sized life, tens of people tending to my needs, big feasts, chauffeurs to drive me around, travel and adventure!'

The huge palace, the official residence of the royal family of Mysore, exhibited a perfect blend of the Hindu, Islamic and Gothic architectural styles and was circled by a colourful garden, filled with numerous flowers and plants. Trivia about the place was written on a tourist information board, which I was reading along with the other visitors.

'Our military also offers a somewhat similar lifestyle,' I said as I continued to read.

'Absolutely!' Hema agreed at once. 'The uniform, the Gypsy with a driver, the dinner parties at the mess—it's almost the same. But it comes at a cost.'

'A cost we're ready to pay, right?' I said, and she smiled.

The next two days after the GD had been busy and tiring. We had appeared for the Group Obstacle Race (GOR), the Individual Obstacles (IO), the Progressive Group Tasks (PGT) and the Half Group Task (HGT) tests, which were conducted by a group testing officer (GTO). An officer of the Indian armed forces is required to face situations that test his/her fitness and qualities in many ways. The aim of the above-mentioned tests is to check the physical stamina, determination, courage, team spirit and cooperativeness of each of the candidates. In the IO test, we were made to go through several sets of obstacles, each carrying different marks based on their level of difficulty. The test had to be completed in the given time constraint, and I was able to finish seven out of the ten obstacles. I had planned to tackle the obstacles in decreasing order of their marks, and the three obstacles that I had left out carried the lowest marks, so I ended up doing fine.

The GOR was more of a fun run, with obstacles like a wall, a net of ropes, tyres and so on, all of which we had to manoeuvre. The candidates were divided into groups of ten, and then two groups at a time were made to race simultaneously. For the PGT, there was a set of obstacles on the ground, and members of a group were made to cross each obstacle according to a set of rules. Also, while crossing these obstacles, they were given a load to carry. Material that would help them cross was provided by the GTO, such as a *balli* (wooden log), a plank and a rope with which to tie the balli or the plank. The difficulty level increased with each obstacle, which is how the task gets its name. Our group was able to complete the task well in time. The HGT was similar to the PGT, and the only difference was that the group was further divided into two more sets. We ended up doing just fine in this task too.

On the evening of the fourth day of our SSB interview, Sqn Ldr Yadav had given us the liberty to go outside the centre and enjoy ourselves. The first place Hema and I headed to was the majestic Mysore Palace. We had planned to spend our evening there and then grab a snack before going back to the centre. Sqn Ldr Yadav had asked everyone to be back before eight.

'Are you up for some filter coffee? Mysore is famous for it,' Hema asked as I finished reading the tourist info board.

'Do you know a place?' I asked.

'Appa had told me about a place that serves the best dosa and filter coffee in Mysore,' an excited Hema said.

After a final glance at the grandeur of the palace, we started walking away from it. Hema had been to Mysore many times before, so she knew her way around the city, and the coffee shop was in the vicinity. Twilight had set in, but we still had an hour to go. 'It feels good to wear these kurtis after four long days,' I said, to which Hema added, 'I couldn't agree more.'

'We've gotten bored of our uniforms in four days! Imagine wearing them for a full decade,' I said. 'If we make it through SSB, that will be our fate.'

'I hadn't thought of that before,' Hema exclaimed.

'I've seen my father spend his entire life following the dress code of the army—getting out of the PT dress in the morning only to get into uniform, wearing the ceremonial uniform and formals for the mess functions and dinner nights and so on,' I added.

'But wearing casuals is a choice, wearing a uniform is a hard-earned privilege, right?' Hema said.

'And I'd choose such a privilege over and over again,' I said. We had reached the coffee shop. It was nothing fancy, just a shop with cement walls and narrow wooden tables and stools. Two teenage boys wearing vests and dhotis ran from table to table, taking orders. The aroma of roasted coffee beans was enchanting. I took a whiff before we occupied a table.

'Two cups of coffee, please,' Hema said, and one of the boys responded with a nod. Her gaze followed the young boy as he ran inside the kitchen to get our order.

'They remind me of my brother,' she said to me with a reminiscing smile.

'How so?' I asked.

'Well, let's just say not all of us are privileged enough,' Hema recounted. 'I come from a family that has seen a lot of struggle. I've seen my Appa wake up every morning and go to work before any of us were awake, only to come back in the night, when we would already be in bed. I've seen my Amma work hard at home, as well as at her workplace. I've seen them sacrificing their needs to tend to their children's demands. As we grew up, our expenses increased. Good education is always costly. So my brother would pick up petty jobs at shops to contribute to our family's finances.' She paused to greet the boy with a smile when the coffee arrived, and then continued, 'I just want to make my family proud.'

'They must already be proud of you,' I said. 'You're taking the SSB interview, one of the toughest in the country. It also means that you've made up your mind to go through the air force's back-breaking training. The choice you've made is reason enough for them to be proud.'

'I know. I just hope I make it,' she said. 'Anyway, what about you, Gunjan? How does it feel to be a privileged child of an army officer?'

I stared at the coffee in my hand. *Was I really privileged?* Her question had brought back a lot of memories.

I didn't have an immediate answer. At the same time, I couldn't deny the fact that I was raised in the best possible environment, had received the best education, had worn the best clothes and had grown up eating whatever I liked, whenever I liked. If all this qualified as privilege, then maybe I was. Of course, Hema would have thought that being an army officer's child must have come with its own privileges: free medical facilities, government accommodation, education rebates, free ration, canteen services and what not. That's how the world looked at army families on the other side of the cantonment's walls. But it all came at a cost, which I had never really given much thought to—not until that moment.

* * *

July 1982

'*The state that was once an island of harmony and prosperity is now stained with blood spilt in communal violence. The communal tragedy began in Amritsar in April, where the Bhindranwale group is gaining influence. Prime Minister Indira Gandhi has shown concern over the worsening situation . . .*' Papaji switched off the radio on hearing this grim headline. 'God, what has happened to our beautiful

Amritsar?' a concerned Maa commented as the radio chatter died away.

Two years had passed since we had left Amritsar. Papaji had been posted to Jabalpur, but our hearts and minds still ached for our beloved city. 'I have a feeling it won't just stop at communal violence,' Papaji commented as he narrowed his eyes behind his big, square spectacles. He was reading something scribbled in his diary. Both of them had been busy since late afternoon, calculating our monthly finances. The setting sun had brought in a golden radiance inside the living room of our row house in the Jabalpur Officers Married Accommodation colony. Fresh evening breeze drafted in from the open windows. It was a relief as the morning drizzle had left the afternoon hot and humid. I could see Maa's worried grimace from the corner of the room, where I was playing with Beauty, our snow-white Pomeranian. Whether the grimace was induced by the disheartening headline or the figures on the calculator, I could not tell. I turned my attention back to Beauty, who kept trying to climb on to my shoulders to play with the ribbons in my plaits.

'Something doesn't add up,' a worried Maa mumbled as she rechecked the calculations. 'There's hardly any savings for this month.' She paused to lower her voice and then whispered, 'And Gunjan's birthday is next month.' I could hear them from where I was sitting.

'I asked you to let me opt for a field posting,' Papaji said in a dispirited tone, still studying the balance sheet in his diary. 'The allowance money that officers are given to serve in high altitudes and tough terrain would have helped.'

'Anshu and Gunju couldn't have lived without you,' Maa said. 'You know how restless and fidgety they get when you leave for even a couple of weeks of temporary duty or exercises.'

'But at least they could have continued to study in St Mary's,' Papaji replied, resting the pen and looking away from his diary. I looked away before Maa could steal a glance at me. Reassured that I wasn't prying on them, she said, 'Kendriya Vidyalaya is equally good. The staff is qualified, and its curriculum is promising. I wouldn't have taken this decision without thinking it through. And the best part is that they can both just cycle and go. No expenses for a school bus.' Maa had gotten Dada and me shifted to Kendriya Vidyalaya before the academic session for my fourth standard and Dada's fifth. Instead of lying to us, Maa had plainly told us that it was getting difficult for them to afford St Mary's. It was not in her nature to hide things from her children. Beating around the bush only brought confusion, she believed. Besides, she always said that children must learn the value of the things that were being given to them.

'You're right,' Papaji said as he stretched his legs. 'We'll also have to cut down on some other expenses.'

'I have a suggestion,' Maa said, and before she could say anything more, Papaji barged in, 'I don't want you to take up a job. We'll start saving. Don't worry.'

'But it won't be just any job,' Maa said in a convincing voice, 'it's what I've always wanted to do. I can get a B.Ed degree in a year, and then I can begin teaching in a school. Wherever you get posted, I can join a school there. God willing, the children and I can start going to the same school. Things will become easy then.'

For a while Papaji simply stared at Maa in admiration, then he broke the silence, 'All right, if that's what you want to do, go ahead.' As if on cue, an agitated Dada, stains of grease on his knickers, stomped into the living room and announced loudly, 'I need a new bicycle now! I'm tired of putting the chain on this one ten times a day.' They both looked at Dada and then at each other before exchanging a smile.

For the next few months, Maa worked her fingers to the bone managing things around the house while pursuing her degree simultaneously. She would get us ready for school, prepare breakfast for us and the dog, make us do our homework and prepare her own lesson plans. Dada and I only made things difficult for her without realizing the ordeal she was going through.

Our incessant demands for snacks were met without any grimace. She would spend the evenings helping us with our homework, and when all of us had gone to sleep, she would burn the midnight oil studying for her classes. Her insurmountable patience never let her get agitated, a fact that I would realize much later in life. All this while, Papaji's savings spree held us in good stead. But it was at the cost of certain things, and all of us had to sacrifice. Our reliance on army-issued rations increased and expenses on extra messing had to be cut down considerably. No expensive clothes for a while, no frequent picnics, no increments on pocket money and no more pets in the house, except Beauty.

However, Dada and I were too young to understand any of this, and we continued to question these new developments. This left us agitated as we would often compare ourselves to the well-off kids in school. As a result, we would often argue with our parents on monetary matters. Immature as we were, we once told our parents that if given a chance, we could show them that we were better at handling finances than them. Instead of scolding us or getting angry, Maa and Papaji came up with a plan to teach us a lesson. They gave us an entire month's salary and told us to run the house for that month. Overconfident and hell-bent on proving our point, we took the amount and started to plan the expenditure. After just ten days, we almost ran out of the money they had given us. We realized our mistake and told Maa and Papaji that we had failed miserably. But instead of being angry or frustrated with us, they were content that their kids had learnt an important lesson. The same lesson would hold us in good stead later in life. I had understood the importance of the hard work Maa had been doing all this while.

As Papaji's tenure at Jabalpur crawled towards an end, Maa was almost done with her degree. One fine night, Maa invited Mrs Gupta, the teacher who had been assessing her lesson plans and assignments, over for dinner. On the same afternoon, Papaji had expressed his discontentment about Mrs Gupta's visit. He didn't like the lady because he felt she was biased and partial. The student marked first in order of merit was supposed to be given a scholarship by the university Maa had enrolled in. But despite Maa's endless efforts and excellent performance, Mrs Gupta had been partial and kept her in second place so another student, her relative, could get the scholarship. Nevertheless, humble as Maa was, she had still invited her in good faith. I had learnt about the whole matter from Dada. This filled the nine-year-old me with a lot of anger and hatred, especially as I strongly believed that the scholarship money would have helped our family. I decided to seek revenge on behalf of my mother.

Maa and Mrs Gupta chatted for a while over snacks before dinner was served. I had insisted that I be allowed to help serve the dinner. That is when I planned my mischief. Knowing that bowls of daal would be served separately, I added red chilli powder to Mrs Gupta's bowl, enough to set her tongue on fire. To make my plan succeed, I didn't keep any water bottle on the table. The first spoonful of daal did its magic, and Mrs Gupta started to squeal. As she rapidly fanned her tongue with her hands, I ran to the kitchen and came back with a glass full of Papaji's white rum. She gulped half of it in a hurry before she realized it wasn't water. Her expression changed; her face blanched and, the next moment, she had thrown up all over the floor! Poor Mrs Gupta would remember that dinner her whole life. I was excused—everyone thought I had mistaken rum for water. After all, the bottle it was kept in was a plain glass bottle. It was then that I discovered how good I was at being mischievous.

We had scrambled out of our financial crisis by the time we moved to Tezpur, Assam, towards the end of 1983. Papaji was posted as an attaché to the General Reserve Engineer Force (GREF). We were again admitted in Kendriya Vidyalaya, where Maa had also managed to get a job as a teacher. Slowly, the lessons I had learnt during a hard times in Jabalpur faded away as I began to enjoy my new school. As I entered the sixth standard,

I came up with a whole list of pranks to play on my friends, classmates and teachers. This, in turn, affected my studies, though I always managed to score average marks on the subjects I was good at. Knowing that my mother was in the same school, and that she would get me out of trouble, I took the subjects I didn't like for granted. I laid my wager on this assumed privilege. One such subject I hated was social science, so much so that I didn't do any homework for the subject for an entire month—May 1984. I didn't care until the subject teacher found out.

'Everyone, take out your homework notebooks and keep them on your table. I'm coming to check them,' Ms Meenakshi, our social science teacher, announced. She was a beautiful middled-aged lady, slim and fair, and was usually dressed in a saree. What I distinctively remember about her is her curly hair, which hung loosely around her shoulders. It was a bright sunny day and the open window of our classroom allowed the fresh air to come inside. Despite the moderate temperature, I began to sweat at the teacher's surprise announcement. As she scribbled something with white chalk on a green board hung on the front wall, I put my mind to task, trying to find a valid-sounding excuse. Even though Ms Meenakshi was mostly polite, I knew it would make her angry to see an entirely empty notebook.

'My . . . my dog tore a few pages out,' I mumbled nervously when she finally reached my desk, but then I gathered confidence and continued, 'I've given it to a stationery shop for rebinding. I promise, Ma'am.' For a while she stared at me, and then said, 'All right, Gunjan, show it to me this Monday. There's still a weekend left. I hope you get your notebook back by then'. As she moved on, my friend sitting behind me, who knew I was bluffing, tugged at my skirt. I turned to high-five her. The day's trouble was over.

Everything was forgotten by the evening. Maa, Dada and I went to the officers' mess ante room, where the other families had gathered too. Papaji was out on a military exercise that would go on for a few weeks. Maa would take us to the ante room quite often so we wouldn't miss Papaji. We spent most of our evenings watching the common television in the ante room of the mess, along with other kids and grown-ups.

Yeh Jo Hai Zindagi, one of the most iconic sitcoms of all time, had become popular in India then, particularly in our cantonment. Nobody liked to miss out on the episodes, which would air on Friday nights. It was my favourite television series, and I would give up anything to watch it. But that particular Friday was full of surprises.

That evening, as we entered the mess, I saw that Ms Meenakshi was also present. She had come to spend the weekend at her colleague's place inside the cantonment. My very first glance at her reminded me of the lie I'd dished out to her in the morning about my social science homework. Dinner was served early, since the show started late in the evening. What happened at dinner wasn't in my best interests that evening. Ms Meenakshi pulled up a chair next to Maa's seat. When I arrived with my plate to take my seat in front of Maa, I stopped mid-stride to see the two of them chatting. I was afraid she would tell Maa about what had happened in the morning.

'Oh, hello Gunjan, come, have a seat,' Ms Meenakshi said on seeing me.

'Good . . . good evening, Ma'am,' I said as I half-heartedly pulled out my chair. Maa's keen eyes noticed my unease. 'Something wrong, beta? Is the food not to your liking?' she asked. I gave her a fake smile.

'Oh, I think I know what could be troubling your daughter,' Ms Meenakshi said at once. 'My presence must have reminded her of her homework notebook. Any child would be troubled if their hard work were eaten by a dog.' Then she turned to me. 'Don't worry Gunjan, if the stationer is taking time to bind the notebook, you can bring it on Tuesday.' Ms Meenakshi got busy with her food after having unknowingly thrown this bomb at me. A confused Maa stared at me and I tried to look away. She had an inkling that I was hiding something. But she chose to wait until dinner was over. All that while, I hoped for a miracle to happen. But my fate was sealed.

Maa motioned to me to meet her outside the ante room when dinner was over. She needed and explanation, and I needed an escape route. 'Did you lie to her?' she asked me as we both stood outside under a streetlight on the pathway leading to the ante room. The sound of crickets chirping filled the air. She had her arms folded, a mark of her seriousness. 'It's nothing you cannot take care of, Maa,' I replied, trying to sound casual and carefree.

'Beauty doesn't go near notebooks. You haven't done your homework, right?' she asked. Her expression was flat, or else I could have gauged her mood. 'I don't like social science, Maa. I don't want to study the subject. Besides, I know you can find a way and get me excused,' I tried to reason with her.

'You thought I would help you get away with it? Is that why you didn't do your homework?' she asked slowly, yet firmly.

'Of course,' I replied rather casually. 'There should be some perks of having my mother in the same school, right? Now, can we go inside? I don't want to miss the episode.'

For a while she just stared at me, without uttering a word. And then she broke her silence. 'Go home.'

I returned a rather confused and questioning stare. 'I said . . . go home. NOW!' she ordered strictly. I could see that she meant what she said, and I could feel her anger. But the episode was about to start, and I was reluctant, so I didn't move. 'Go home, Gunjan Saxena,' she said for a third time. Maa never repeated anything—ever. If she asked for something and we didn't do it, she would never ask again. But she had asked me to go home, thrice now. There was no way I wasn't going to comply, however reluctant I was. Helpless tears trickled down my face and I stomped away from the ante room angrily. Maa followed me. I ran straight to my room and fell on my bed. By this time, I was sobbing loudly. Maa stood at my room's entrance. It pained her heart to see me cry, but she stuck to being strict.

'Finish your homework now and be prepared to submit the notebook by Monday. Until then, you do not get to go out of this room,' she said and walked away. It only added to my frustration and I lay on the bed, crying. The brimming well of tears dried up after a while, and, besides, I had accepted my fate. Maa came in with a glass of warm milk after half an hour. I didn't look at her—I was still angry. She sat by my side as I scribbled in my notebook. She could see my eyes were still swollen and red. Her hand slowly reached for my face, but I looked away and she pulled it back. She opened the notebook and started to go through its contents. For the rest of the night, I did my pending homework and Maa helped me. Neither of us slept until four in the morning. The next two days were no different. We didn't speak about anything other than my homework. Maa kept bringing the meals and other things I needed to my room, and I kept scribbling. I would cry in between, whenever my hand hurt from all the writing. Maa would write on my behalf for a while then. But she didn't excuse me at all. Eventually, on Monday morning, my homework notebook was ready. 'Promise me you will confess to Ms Meenakshi that you lied, and you will assure her you won't lie again,' Maa said to me as I walked out of the house for school. I didn't turn to look at her. Dada tried to explain to me why Maa had been so strict. The previous year, when Dada had told a lie about spending elsewhere the money given to him for a book, Maa had treated him the same way. His pocket allowance was cut off and he was shown no mercy. *If you do something wrong, intentionally or unintentionally, don't try to hide it with a lie. If you tell the truth, we will not get mad at you, we will always help you,* Maa had told him back then. Later, when I showed my homework notebook to Ms Meenakshi and confessed to her, she made the entire class applaud. She was happy that I had displayed such determination and integrity. Honestly, it filled me with pride; it was an incident I would remind myself of often in future. When I reached home that afternoon, I waited for Maa. When she finally returned from school, I ran straight to her and hugged her. There were tears in her eyes and in mine. I had learnt my lesson. The upcoming Friday, we didn't have to go to the officers' mess to watch our favourite sitcom. Maa bought a television for us from her savings—a Weston CRT colour television. Her children had earned it, she would say. Besides, having a television at home saved a lot of time that was wasted travelling to the mess. She wanted us to dedicate the time to our studies, to subjects that needed attention. I dedicated it to social science. When Papaji came home the next week, Maa filled him in on everything he had missed. He was amazed and proud at the fact that I hadn't broken down under pressure, even at such a young age. 'You must know, Gunju, your parents work really hard to make sure you and Anshu get everything,' Papaji said to me one night, when he came to my room to wish me goodnight after dinner. 'Maa has sacrificed her own wants to fulfil her children's needs. Sacrifice and hard work reap honest and great results. Maa and I believe you and Anshu will make us proud one day. To be able to do so, sometimes you will have to get out of your comfort zone and accept challenges. And remember, never seek shortcuts, never seek privilege, never do anything dishonourable. You must earn everything you get. There's a different taste to it, a taste of satisfaction.' Then he kissed me goodnight on my forehead and left. But I spent the rest of the night thinking about what Papaji had told me.

* * *

We managed to get back at the SSB centre on time. Preparation for the personal interview, which was scheduled the next day, was going on in full swing inside our barracks. But Hema and I hit the bed as soon as we entered the barracks. 'You had asked me a question at the coffee shop,' I turned to Hema as I lay in bed.

'Which question?' She had clearly forgotten.

'You had asked how it feels to be a privileged child of an army officer,' I reminded her.

'And . . . ?' she said.

'Well, it feels great,' I said happily.

I turned to the other side and slept content, leaving a confused Hema with her thoughts.

SEVEN

Job interviews are generally tailored to judge how well the interviewee can convince the interviewer that he or she is fit for the job. It is even more challenging when the interviewer is hell-bent on finding a good reason to deem the candidate unfit. How do you convince them in such a situation? The answer is—with honesty. That is what is required in the personal interviews of the SSB exam, according to Papaji. He would tell me that if I missed even one of the prerequisite qualities, the armed forces would not even consider my candidature; it would not put the lives of its men and women at risk just because someone like me would lose a job opportunity. So making sugar-coated statements wasn't going to help at all. If one is not chosen, it's better to accept the inevitable rather than feel disheartened, prepare well and execute better in the next SSB exam. On the morning of the fifth day, just before the personal interviews were to commence, I promised myself I would not crib or cry if I failed—I would accept the results calmly and go back like a true fighter.

'I wonder if we'll get tickets to go back home tonight, in case we don't get recommended?' Deepa asked. We were all sitting in rows outside the conference hall, waiting for the interviews to begin. There were two bulbs fitted to sockets above the hall's door, one red and one green. The red one was glowing, indicating an interview was in progress inside.

'You think you won't make it?' I asked Deepa in a hushed tone.

'We can't be too sure, can we?' she replied.

'It's all about being confident,' Aditi said. 'I've only shown them what they needed to see. There's no chance I'm going back today without a yes.'

'Such overconfidence!' Hema couldn't keep herself from commenting. Aditi rolled her eyes detestably. 'If I can see it, surely they can too,' Hema said to me faintly. 'I can bet a wager on her rejection.'

I had my eyes fixed on the bulbs. As soon as the green one glowed, I'd be only one candidate away from my interview. I looked at my attire for the day—my pants and shirt were neatly ironed, my hair was tied in a tight bun. I cleared my throat. I was set. And as if on cue, the green light flashed.

As soon as the interviewee went inside, the light turned from green to red. My gaze was fixed on the bulb. It must have been less than ten minutes, but it felt like an eternity before the candidate came out. She seemed relaxed. After about another two minutes, the green bulb lit up again. I could feel my heart flutter as I stood up to go in. Hema wished me luck and I smiled back at her. I pulled open the door of the conference room and, just as I had imagined, I saw in front of me a panel of six officers sitting behind a rounded table. They were all familiar faces I had encountered during our various tests.

'May I come in?' I asked.

'Please be seated,' Wing Commander Pathak signalled. He was the interviewing officer (IO) I had seen during the PABT.

I seated myself on the edge of the chair, both my hands carefully folded on my lap. Sqn Ldr Yadav and Sqn Ldr Virk smiled at me. I was too nervous to smile back. The others were busy going through the files that had been kept in front of them. I guessed it was my personal information questionnaire form, which each of us had filled up on the first day of the SSB. I patiently waited for the IO to shoot the first question.

'How was your SSB experience, Ms Saxena?' he finally lifted his head and asked.

'Informative, Sir,' I replied at once, 'and memorable.'

'How many friends did you make here?' he asked.

'I've interacted with all the other candidates, and I plan to keep in touch with them, Sir, regardless of how things pan out,' I replied. I didn't want them to think I was partial and avoided telling them that Hema was the only one I could call a 'friend' there. But the truth was that I had interacted with all of them. The IO then asked me basic questions about my family and education. The more I talked, the more relaxed I felt. But there was one question that made me stop and think for a while.

'Tell us why you want to join the Indian Air Force?'

I knew the answer to this question. I had prepared for it all my life. What I did not know was how to frame my answer. Should I sound passionate? What if I sounded desperate instead? How could I tackle this? What should I say to convince them? There was no time to plan or prepare. I had to be quick.

* * *

September 1984

The road to Etawah was shining wet from a fresh drizzle. Papaji and I were riding a scooter he had borrowed from a course mate in Jhansi. Beauty had given birth to a litter and all of us wanted the pups to go to caring and responsible families. So Papaji had taken it upon himself to deliver them to some of his acquaintances who were willing to adopt them. The last of the litter was travelling with us to his new home in the scooter's front basket. We had stopped by a roadside tea stall to keep ourselves from getting wet in the drizzle. I didn't want the puppy to catch a fever. It was asleep on my lap while Papaji and I sipped tea from earthen cups; a mixed aroma of hot tea and rain-washed earth perfumed the air. It had stopped raining and we had to reach our destination before sundown, so we finished our tea and got up to get going after paying the chaiwallah.

Just then, we heard the shutter of a nearby garage opening. Papaji paused midway into kick-starting his scooter as something inside the garage caught his eye. He put the scooter back on the stand and started to walk towards the garage. I trotted behind him, holding the puppy in my arms. He paused in front of the garage and anchored his gaze on a light-blue vintage car.

'What is the matter, Papaji?' I asked, breaking the silence.

'You see that car?' he said excitedly, and I nodded. 'It's a 1951 Studebaker Champion! One of my favourites.'

Confusion puckered my brows. 'So?' I asked.

'So,' he smiled at me and looked back at the car, 'I want to buy it.'

'But it's an old car!' I exclaimed.

'It's a bullet-nose vintage beauty, Gunju,' he said. 'Do you know it's a limited-edition car with a spinner-grille?

There's a difference between "old" and "vintage".' He then walked up to the mechanic inside the garage and asked him if the car was for sale. I stood there, wondering if he actually meant to buy it. The mechanic told him the car belonged to His Highness, the Maharaja of Gwalior, Madhavrao Scindia. He came back to me and said, 'Let's go.'

'Yes, let's go, who wants to buy an old car anyway?' I said. I thought he had given up.

He kick-started the scooter and said, 'We're going to meet the maharaja.'

His Highness lived in the Jai Vilas Palace in Gwalior— the residence of the descendants of the Maratha Scindia dynasty, part of which had been converted into a museum in 1964. When we got on the road leading to the front gate of the palace, a huge white building came into view. The road was lined with beautifully trimmed trees and hedges. There were other tourists going in the same direction, probably to see the museum. As we got closer, I could see the beautiful European architecture of the stunning three-storey grand edifice. There was a round marble fountain in front of the main gate. Papaji parked his scooter in the visitors' parking spot, and we walked towards the main gate. Upon enquiring from the guards, Papaji learnt that the maharaja was available at his residence, but nobody was allowed inside the premises. Papaji insisted on meeting him, saying the maharaja wouldn't deny him permission once he learnt that an army officer had come with a special request. Papaji was hell-bent on meeting him and I could see there was no way he was going to back off. The guards could see it too, so they did as they were asked. To their surprise and to mine, the maharaja told them not to keep an army officer waiting outside, and we were quickly escorted in. We entered the residential property; it was even more beautiful from the inside. The Italian marble flooring, ornate accessories, lavish Persian carpets, shining chandeliers and rare antiquities from various parts of the world, displayed along the pathways, were mesmerizing. We were taken to a small garden, where chairs had already been laid out for us to sit on. Stewards worked carefully to place silver crockery, including cups, saucers and a teapot, on a small round glass table. We were asked to sit and wait there. In another two minutes, the maharaja came to meet us. Papaji stood up and I imitated him. His Highness shook hands with Papaji.

'Thank you for letting us in,' Papaji said.

'It is my honour to have an army officer in my residence,' replied the humble and charming maharaja who was dressed in an embroidered white kurta pyjama. 'Let's have a cup of tea before we discuss what brings you here.'

I had imagined someone wearing an enormous crown on his head and a bundle of necklaces jangling on his torso.

But he had a shaved face, neatly cut hair and was wearing a pair of spectacles. His plain manners complemented his reputation.

'So what bothers you, Major?' he asked Papaji after the basic introductions were dealt with.

'I want to buy a car that once belonged to you,' Papaji replied plainly. As if having a cup of tea with the maharaja was not enough. If I had been in his place, I would have dropped all my other wishes. But I was amazed at Papaji's determination and straightforwardness. The maharaja was rather amused.

'You have come all the way on your scooter to buy a car that belongs to me?' he said with a smile. 'Why?'

'Because it's a rare model and it belongs to you,' Papaji replied honestly. 'I'm talking about the 1951 Studebaker Champion I saw at a garage.'

'Oh, that one,' His Highness said. 'Forgive me, but I can't sell that one. I have a collection of other cars you can choose from.' I thought it was a generous deal and that Papaji should take it. 'Besides, a car is a car.'

'I beg to differ, Your Highness,' Papaji said. 'The 1951 V-6 engine, the improved camshaft, the longer wheelbase, the massive 85 horsepower at 4000 rpm, all of it makes this car more than just another car. I apologize if I'm being imprudent, Your Highness, but I don't want to buy any other car,' Papaji said. 'It's okay if you can't sell it.'

The maharaja stared at Papaji for a moment. I could hear the stewards whispering to each other. Papaji must have annoyed him, I thought. But the maharaja only smiled and continued to sip tea from his cup. Nobody talked about the car any more. I enjoyed a plate full of fruit cake, which was arranged for me on His Highness's orders. The puppy ran around the garden carefree. After half an hour of this royal rendezvous, Papaji took his permission to leave. The humble Maharaja insisted on seeing us off. Just as we reached the gate, the maharaja asked out of the blue, 'Do you really want to buy that car?'

'I do,' Papaji replied. 'I'll arrange for the payment. I can pay it in instalments but I will pay whatever the cost is.'

'I can give it to you on one condition, and no questions will be asked,' the maharaja said. Papaji waited for him to speak, and he continued, 'I will take a payment of one rupee only.' My jaw dropped. The maharaja looked at me and said, 'And if you allow me to keep the puppy.' Flabbergasted, I looked at Papaji, who nodded his approval. I kissed the puppy and passed it into the maharaja's open hands. Papaji at once took out a one-rupee note from his wallet and handed it to the maharaja. 'The car will reach your address tomorrow. This is the least I can do for our brave men in uniform who keep us all safe,' a smiling maharaja said as he stroked the puppy's head.

Papaji thanked him and we left. I was overwhelmed by the exceptional turn of events that I had just witnessed. A simple, plain and honest confrontation had reaped extraordinary results. And yet, the chances were taken with utmost sincerity—something I wasn't ever going to forget. Over the next few years, we would undertake memorable long journeys in that wonderful car, along with our dogs. We would camp on the way whenever possible. And I would always wonder how Papaji was able to convince the maharaja.

* * *

It doesn't take much to convince someone of anything if you actually mean what you say. Honesty, grit and determination can move mountains, and I had seen it. When the IO asked me why I wanted to join the Indian Air Force, I had a couple of answers ready for him. I could have sounded passionate; I could have sounded patriotic or even adamant, corny and desperate. But I knew why I had come for this. I knew what I wanted and why I wanted it. I knew what to tell them.

'I want to fly,' I replied without thinking it over. While all the others stared at me, I kept my eyes on the IO.

'Why do you want to fly in the Indian Air Force?' he asked. 'You could have also opted for civil aviation.'

'There's a lot of investment in civil aviation courses, and no job security,' I replied honestly. Civil aviation, especially private scheduled airlines in the 1990s, was still in its nascent stage in India. And the fee for a flying course was skyrocketing with every passing day. 'But if I join the Indian Air Force, I'll be commissioned in one and a half years, and that, too, as a gazetted officer of this country. Plus, I like the less-than-ordinary lifestyle in defence services.'

The IO then flipped through the pages of a file kept in front of him.

'How is your general knowledge, Ms Saxena?' he asked.

'Below average,' I replied. 'It's not good.'

'Why? Don't you listen to the news or read newspapers?' he asked.

'I read magazines, mostly about Bollywood, Sir,' I replied. Everyone smiled at my answer.

'But you must tell us something important that has been in the news currently,' the IO said. I strained my memory and tried to think.

'Umm . . . Sushmita Sen got crowned Miss Universe recently,' I replied. The IO chuckled.

'Anyway . . . how do you plan to lose weight if we recommend you?' he asked. It was a valid question. I was overweight according to Indian Air Force standards.

Any other civilian would consider me fit, but this was the Indian Air Force, and they were looking for leaner and meaner air warriors.

'My father will help me lose weight with regular physical training,' I replied, and since they knew I was the daughter of an army officer, they knew my father would see to it that I did sweat and burn it off. You cannot outmatch a 'fauji' when it comes to physical training.

'All right, that will be all,' the IO said. 'Please wait outside for the results. We wish you luck.'

An hour passed and impatience got the better of me. To divert my mind, I paced the corridor, while everyone around me discussed and reassessed their performance. Even when I tried to think, I could not recall the sequence of events that had happened inside. I almost forgot my answers to the IO's questions. Did I use too many gestures? Did I even move my hands? Was I sitting straight? Did I blink too much? Was my leg shaking? I could not remember anything. One after another, the candidates kept going in and coming out. By lunchtime, all the interviews were over. The red bulb lit up again. Another countdown! I started to think about my dogs. Their memories made me smile and I felt better. But the feeling lasted only until Sqn Ldr Yadav came out with a page in his hand. I could feel my heart pounding in my chest. All of us sat in our chairs quietly and waited for him to speak.

'After compiling the results of the tests,' he announced, 'I'd like to tell you that all of you cleared the PABT exam.' The girls looked at each other. The suspense still lingered. 'But to everyone's hard luck, there's only one candidate the board has recommended today.' No sooner had he said this than my face dropped. *It's definitely not going to be me.* But I wanted it to be.

'Chest Number 4,' Sqn Ldr Yadav announced, his eyes scanning the crowd and stopping at me. I partially raised my right hand. 'Congratulations, you've made it!' Sqn Ldr Yadav said. 'Please meet me in my office. The others may leave. I wish you all the very best of luck.'

A wave of chatter swept across the crowd that had already started to disperse. But I quietly sat there, still trying to let it sink in. Nobody congratulated me, except for Hema. 'So you get to fly,' she said, trying hard to hide her own disappointment at not being recommended. 'Congratulations, Gunjan.'

I hugged her. I was elated at my selection, yet sad that Hema had to go.

'Here's my telephone number,' Hema said, handing me a piece of paper. 'Call me when you come for medicals at IAM [Institute of Aerospace Medicine] in Bangalore. We'll catch up. Now hurry up and go to Manoj Sir's office.'

We hugged each other, and she left. Sqn Ldr Yadav informed me that my medical tests were scheduled to be held at IAM Bangalore, the same place where Hema's mother worked in the administration wing. I was directed to an office where I was asked to fill up certain forms. My ticket to Bangalore was handed to me before I was freed for lunch. I ran straight to the STD booth and informed my parents of the result.

'Everything I ever believed has been proven right,' said an elated Papaji.

EIGHT

Until then, I was still trying to find a purpose to my existence. But after seeing myself standing all alone in the entire barracks as the recommended candidate, I understood it. Getting recommended was only the beginning. The path to glory was strewn with obstacles, ones that would almost break me.

I spent a lonely night in the barracks the day I was recommended, but I enjoyed a dreamless slumber. The next morning, a Jeep dropped me to the railway station. I reached Bangalore in the afternoon, where another military vehicle had been arranged to drop me to IAM. IAM Bangalore, a premier institute of the Indian Air Force and the hub of aerospace medicine activities in the country, is the only institute of its kind in South Asia for conducting a doctor of medicine (MD) course in aerospace medicine for aircrew, medical officers and paramedics. Upon reaching IAM, I saw that it was a typical air force white-and-sky-blue building with neatly trimmed trees and grass gardens in front. The tricolour was hoisted on a flagpole in front of the building. An attendant took me to their 'trinity mess'; a big dorm room was allotted to me, where I was told that I would be the only occupant for the next few days—no other SSB medical tests had been scheduled during that time. It felt lonely and depressing to not have any company in such a place. I was told to report to the medical officer's office first thing the next morning. As soon as I finished lunch, I went straight to the PCO booth and called Hema.

'Why are you staying there?' Hema said when I told her I had reached IAM. 'Come stay with us, at our place.'

'No, no, I don't want to trouble . . .' But before I could finish, she barged in, 'No, I won't listen to anything. You have to come and stay with us.'

'But is it even allowed?' I asked her.

'I'll have Amma speak to the concerned officer,' Hema said excitedly.

'All right then, see you tomorrow,' I said and hung up.

That evening I was told to fill up some papers regarding my medical history, which I then had to carry the next morning, before my medical tests. Spending the night in that big dorm room was made easy by the attendant, who kindly set up the common room's television there for me to watch. As always, Bollywood songs lulled me to sleep.

The initial few medical tests, including a blood sample, blood-pressure check and other physical measurements and inspections, were over by noon, and I was free for the day. By this time, Hema's mother had already asked the medical officer for his permission to allow me to stay with them. A willingness application filled out by me had to be submitted, which I did, after which I was allowed to go—on the condition that I would not be late for the tests the next day. I got free earlier than Hema's mother, so I took the local bus for Jayanagar, the place where Hema stayed, not very far from the city centre. When I entered Jayanagar, I saw that unlike the commercial hub that Bangalore was, Jayanagar still maintained the old charm of the city. Apart from some shops, the place was mostly residential. I pushed open the bus's window to let the soothing afternoon breeze in. I was excited to finally get to Hema's house.

I got off the bus at the place Hema had told me to. Finding her house wasn't difficult. Among the rows of all the other two-storey houses adjacent to a narrow street, numbered in ascending order, I found myself standing with my bag outside Hema's house in no time. I rang the bell, wearing a huge smile on my face.

No sooner had Hema opened the door than she hugged me, throwing all her weight on me, almost screaming in excitement. A boy came and took my bag in while she pulled me inside.

'He's my little brother,' Hema said.

'Namaskara,' the little boy, whose name I couldn't catch, greeted me. I greeted him back. While her brother went inside with my luggage, Hema walked me through the house. It was a small, old-fashioned home with family pictures hanging on almost all the walls. Hema showed me her room, and we chatted for a while before she prepared two cups of coffee for the both of us. Her mother reached home by six in the evening and greeted me warmly. She began preparations for dinner at once. After almost two hours, we were all seated at the dining table. It was for the first time that Hema introduced me to her father, who had just joined us from work. Gentle in behaviour and soft-spoken, he was a medium-built man dressed in loose trousers, a shirt and sandals, sporting a thick moustache. While Hema's mother arranged mouth-watering delicacies on the dining table, Hema and I shared our SSB experience with everyone. Mirth and laughter filled the room. Traditional home-cooked food only added to the warmth and love. After a long time, I felt at home and wondered when I would be able to dine like this with my own family again.

Hema's mother woke me up the next morning. 'You must catch the six o'clock bus to reach IAM on time,' she said to me as she offered me some coffee. 'I've packed idli and gunpowder chutney for breakfast.' I hugged her at this heart-warming gesture. 'Thank you, Aunty.' She smiled and hugged me back.

Hema's mother was right about the timings. The six o'clock bus dropped me at IAM by half past seven and I was ready for my medical tests by eight. The tests were carried out and they were all done by noon. A medical board was held thirty minutes later and I was summoned to the conference hall. It was to be chaired by the commandant, with two other medical officers. When I went in, the commandant broke the first awful news to me. I had received a 'temporary rejection', or TR, for being overweight by 7 kg. But I was already prepared for this. I was given four weeks to lose the extra weight, after which I was supposed to go to the Air Force Central Medical Establishment (AFCME) in Delhi for an appeal to the medical board, where my weight would be rechecked, as per the commandant's directions. But this wasn't the worst part. The minimum required height for a female officer for flying was 162.5 cm. When they told me that I was only 161.5 cm and therefore eligible only for ground duty and not flying, I almost cried in disappointment. But then, the commandant told me that I still had a chance, for an appeal medical board would hear this rejection as well. It didn't help to lift my spirits but I listened to him carefully. Everything had been going so well, and then suddenly I was being told that I wasn't eligible to fly! All my dreams came crashing down. The only reason I had chosen to become an officer in the Indian Air Force was because I wanted to fly. And knowing that I would never fly, just because of a mere centimetre, was very upsetting. The moment the board handed over my documents and dismissed me, I ran straight to the PCO and dialled home.

'Don't fret, Gunju, just come back home,' he said after I told him about the board's decision. 'We will figure this out. You still have an appeal medical board.'

'But Papa, I can't increase my height,' I said, upset.

'You just come home, beta. We'll figure everything out,' he said. 'You came all this way and got recommended on your very first attempt. You passed all your tests. You were excellent at the PABT. You cannot let one centimetre decide your fate. You're meant to fly, I just know you are. For now, just come home. We miss you.' Still wondering what would happen and how, I hung up and started for Hema's house.

Hema left no stone unturned to cheer me up when I told her everything. 'Amma told me that there have been cases where up to two centimetres of difference have been waived off for male candidates. I'm sure the appeal medical board will yield positive results,' she said.

'Losing weight is possible. But there's no way I can increase my height,' I said.

'You might never have to,' Hema said. 'Cheer up now! At least you're still getting a chance to wear the uniform. Rejoice in this fact. Let's go for dinner.'

The next morning, I boarded my train to Avadi in Chennai and reached home by afternoon. Papaji had come to pick me up. All this while, I had dealt with mixed feelings, consumed by both joy and gloom. But everyone else was happy and proud that I had been recommended in my first SSB interview and kept cheering me. Maa had made aloo paranthas—my favourite—but I had lost all appetite.

'Don't worry, you can eat today. We'll work on your weight loss from tomorrow,' Papaji consoled me.

'I always told you she was fat and lazy,' Dada commented rather playfully.

'Not in the mood, Dada,' I retorted. Dada went back to eating his paranthas.

'It's just a few kilos,' Maa said.

'It's not about my weight, Maa,' I said in frustration. I was reminded of the possibility that I might never be eligible to fly. I thought it better to get up and go to my room than spread more pessimism around the dining table.

Knowing that I would have to spend the next four weeks in uncertainty added to my frustration. If that wasn't all, I had almost started to believe I *actually* was unfit to fly. Weight can be lost, but height cannot be gained, especially at my age. A cycle of negative thoughts was set in motion. Visions of spending my service days, if at all I was allowed to join the forces, on the ground started to storm my mind. Tears of disappointment trickled down my face as I lay in my bed.

'So you've given up already?' Papaji said as he stood by the door. I dug my face deeper into the pillow. He came and sat by my side, placing his hand gently on my head.

'You're going to wear a uniform soon,' he said. 'Men and women in uniform do not know how to give up. Besides, these little hurdles are part of your SSB interview. The Indian Air Force wants to know how resolute you are before they offer you command over their men and machines.' I had almost stopped crying. He continued, 'Once you wear the rank, you'll come across situations that will break you. There's no shame in falling, but there is no glory in not trying to get up after the fall. You may have to go to war. Wars are unforgiving. What will you do then? In the last few metres during a run, every single drop of blood matters, every bit of energy matters, every stride matters. Winners aren't those who put all their effort into the beginning of the run; winners are those who do not give up in the last few metres. Now, you must understand that you're running the last few metres. Do you want to see yourself win?'

I slowly turned and looked at Papaji. There was a smile on his face, a smile I remember even to this day. He was clearly proud of his daughter—he had said it so many times that day. He had telephoned his course mates and bragged about me getting recommended. My recommendation was a milestone achievement for my parents. He was happy and I didn't want to spoil the day for him. 'I will try my best,' I said and hugged him.

That night as I slept, Papaji chalked out a four-week diet plan for me. My diet was suddenly shifted from paranthas, butter chicken and rotis to fruits, salads, low carbohydrates and curd, and lots of water. Not only this, he even planned my daily physical-training regimen. Never in my life had it occurred to me that I might have to diet someday. And for the food lover that I was, it was going to be one hell of a ride. It did not affect only me, but my entire family had to shift to eating salads and food that was low in calories. Maa thought that it might affect my morale if they all ate regular food while I survived on salads.

Papaji woke me up at half past four the next morning and took me for a run, almost against my will. I started panting after only a few minutes, but Papaji kept motivating me. 'At least finish a kilometre today, and then we'll gradually increase the distance,' he said.

After an exhausting morning session, I was given plain vegetable salad without salt for breakfast. Somehow, I managed to swallow the tasteless veggies. It went to Maa's heart to see me suffer but Dada seemed quite amused. 'If only you had listened to me and exercised regularly,' he commented. The morning took a toll on me and added to my frustration. If that wasn't all, Papaji's unit juniors—two captains and a lieutenant—called on Papaji during lunch.

In line with the age-old traditions of the army, Maa and Papaji had to succumb to every demand of the guests. As a result, a plethora of cuisines was prepared for lunch, including some of my favourites. As I sat there, my face as long as a fiddle, while everyone enjoyed drinks, Maa offered starters to the guests.

'Won't Gunjan eat her favourite kebabs?' one of the officers asked Maa when she passed by me without offering me any.

'She's on a weight-loss regime,' Papaji answered. 'She got recommended and now she has to lose weight to clear her medical tests.'

'Congratulations' came in unison, and I replied with a forced but humble smile. Mouth-watering snacks kept on coming while I sat there, almost depressed at not being able to eat any of it. I could have made it through if I was allowed to go to my room but Maa thought it would be disrespectful to do so. Finally, when lunch was laid out on the table and everyone filled their plates, when the smell of hot butter chicken and malai kofta reached my nostrils, I broke down. Without saying a word, I got up and sped into my room, leaving behind an embarrassed Papaji. I just could not take it any more. When the guests left, Papaji came to my room.

'Is this your best?' he asked calmly. I looked the other way.

'You said you'll try your best,' he said.

'I can't do it,' I said, without looking at him, 'when everybody else enjoys eating my favourite food in front of me.'

'But it's just for a few weeks,' Papaji said.

'You don't understand, Papaji, I've never been on diet for even half a day in my life,' I retorted. 'I hate it.'

'Then how do we solve this problem?' he asked.

'I don't know,' I replied in frustration.

'I . . . I think I know,' he said. 'We've done it once, we'll do it again.'

* * *

December 1986

'I don't want to eat,' I said as we all seated ourselves at the dinner table.

'Why? What happened?' Maa asked as she passed the pickle to Dada.

'She misses Beauty,' Dada filled in for me. 'I miss her too.'

'I want to go back to Jammu,' I said melancholically. Beauty was buried in the backyard of our accommodation in Jammu. She had left us five months after Papaji had been posted to Jammu in March that year. Whenever I missed Beauty, I'd go and sit in the backyard. But I couldn't do so here in Vadodara, where Papaji had come to attend a course for over seven months.

'Or maybe we can get another dog?' Dada suggested.

'No more pets until we get posted out of here,' Maa said at once.

'But you must not disrespect the sanctity of a family dinner,' Papaji said to me. 'Eat your food.'

'But I'm not hungry at all,' I said. 'I feel sick.'

'It's okay,' Maa said to me, and then turned to Papaji. 'She'll feel better in the morning.'

I hardly had a nibble that evening, and went to sleep. I could not understand whether it was my grief or if I was actually sick. In the early hours of the morning, I woke up with a high fever and nausea. Before I could scramble out of bed to rush to bathroom, I threw up on the floor. The loud retching woke Maa up and she came running to my room, only to see me standing before a puddle of vomit, looking embarrassed. 'It's okay, don't worry about it,' she said and tied my fluffy hair up into a ponytail before

My sixteenth birthday at Pathankot

At the Chennai railway station, when I was leaving to join my unit in Udhampur,
clicked by Papaji. Sherry and Crazy (the dogs) can be seen too

My family and I during my passing-out parade, clicked by
Wing Commander R.O.J. Assey

At my passing-out parade. Papaji and my instructor,
Wing Commander R.O.J. Assey

Receiving the Minoo Engineer Trophy for first in order of merit

Reviewing officer Air Chief Marshal Latif (retd) putting wings on our uniform
as white epaulettes are removed

At the Jungle and Snow Survival Camp during one of the treks

On our way to the Jungle Survival Camp

During the Jungle and Snow Survival Camp (trekking)

Post Kargil. Clicked for an article in the *Savvy* magazine

Papaji with Dada, when he was a cadet in the Indian Military Academy, Dehradun

On the evening prior to the passing-out parade, with Maa, Dada and Papaji

Papaji and I at the Bagdogra crew room

With Papaji in a Cheetah helicopter at the Bagdogra air force station

Maa and Papaji visiting me at the Bagdogra air force station

From left: Anuradha, me and Srividya with the HPT-32 aircraft towards the end of the first term at the Air Force Academy, Dundigal

My course mates and I, with Wing Commander S.S. Patil (CFI), towards the end of the first term

I could rush to the bathroom. After I had thrown up thrice in an hour, I was taken to the military hospital without delay. I felt so weak I could hardly walk to the car. I had been feeling sick for a week now, but careless as I was, I had just taken a paracetamol tablet every day rather than tell my parents about my worsening condition, afraid that I would be given injections. Injections scared the soul out of me. But I had no choice that day.

The medical officer checked my pulse rate and flashed a small torch in my eyes, after which I was told to furnish a blood sample. I looked at Papaji with terror-filled eyes. Before he could say anything, the nursing assistant (NA) pricked my finger with a needle. The blood sample was taken care of, thanks to the NA's nimbleness. But then the real horror came, when I overheard the medical officer prescribing some injections. My heart sank.

'I'll take any medicine they give me, but no injections. Please,' I pleaded, teary-eyed.

'But you're very weak, Gunju, the injections are necessary. It's okay, I'm with you,' he tried to make me understand.

But I was already panicking. I would have fled if I had the energy to run. But I sat in the wheelchair, helpless. When we entered the injection room, the NA made me sit on an inclined chair and asked me to place my arm on the armrest. Half reluctantly, I followed his instructions but kept looking at Papaji with pleading, tear-filled eyes.

'It'll be over before you know it,' he said. All hell broke loose when I caught a glimpse of a big, pointy syringe as the NA prepared the first injection.

'No, please, Papaji, no injection,' I whimpered. After another moment, I was literally screaming.

'Listen to me,' Papaji said, quite loudly, and my whining tuned down to a sob. He then gently held my hand, cupped my chin and said, 'It'll be just one small prick. You won't even feel it. I promise. Trust me . . . just a small prick.'

'You're lying,' I said faintly.

'Get the first injection and see for yourself,' Papaji said.

'No,' I mumbled, 'first you get one. I want to see how they do it.' The NA chuckled at this. Papaji sighed.

'I can show you someone else who might be getting an injection right now,' the NA suggested. A loud 'no' was my reply.

'It's okay,' Papaji turned to the NA and said, 'You give me some injection, something like an anti-tetanus or something.'

Amazed by this strange agreement, the NA prepared an injection for Papaji. I stopped crying and focused on the process. I saw the NA tapping on Papaji's arm to find the right vein. As he brought the syringe closer to Papaji's skin, I leaned forward for a closer look. The moment the syringe pushed its way inside Papaji's skin and the NA drew some blood, I shifted my gaze to Papaji. His face was expressionless, as if nothing had happened. No twitching of muscles—just a plain face. When the process was over, he turned to me and said, 'See, nothing happened. You're scared for no reason.'

I agreed to get the injections. I did feel the prick, but it was not as painful as I had imagined. The good part was that after this little success of mine, Papaji treated me to a cassata ice-cream. As we ate spoonfuls, we laughed at my fear of injections, which was now a thing of the past. He had proved to me that it was simple and, therefore, possible. I do not fear injections any more.

* * *

The next morning, Papaji woke me up and took me to his unit's PT ground, where his entire regiment had lined up in threes for their regular morning PT session. I stood in a corner while Papaji marched to the front. A young officer, dressed in white shorts and a white T-shirt—standard PT rig—received a report from the subedar major and then reported to Papaji, as everyone else stood in attention. 'Two hundred and thirty-five jawans, fourteen junior commissioned officers (JCOs) and three officers for the morning PT parade, Sir. May I have the permission to march them off?' To this, Papaji, being the second-in-command of his unit and also the officer-in-charge for training, replied, 'Please go ahead.' After the reporting procedure was over, everyone marched off for the morning run. Papaji took me in the opposite direction for the run. He ran ahead of me and I followed; he did as many push-ups as he made me do; he cycled for five kilometres and I followed; he did every exercise that I was supposed to do, and I followed his lead. When we reached home, exhausted, he took me to the storeroom and started to look for something. As I watched in confusion, he fished out an old edition of *Reader's Digest* from a pile of old newspapers and magazines. With a victorious smile under his thick moustache, he blew the dust off its cover.

'What is it?' I asked.

'It's our diet plan for the next four weeks,' he said. As we went into the living room, he turned a few pages of the magazine and handed it to me. It had the diet routine for Rekha—one of Bollywood's most iconic actors.

'So you want me to follow her diet?' I asked as I read through the page.

'We,' he stressed the word, '*we* will be following Rekha's diet.'

'What?' I reacted. 'Why do you need to diet?'

'I can't let my Gunju diet alone,' he said. 'Besides, it'll be good for me to lose some extra kilos as well.' He then looked at Maa, who had just entered the living room, and continued, '. . . And impress your Maa.' Maa smiled and went into the kitchen.

The diet plan from *Reader's Digest* was not as strict as the one Papaji had chalked out before. And having someone by my side, eating the same food as me, was quite motivating. Having Papaji accompany me in everything for these four tough weeks was a big help. We ran together, cycled together, ate together, and all of this helped me reach my desired weight. Each week was tougher than the previous one. My runs were timed, my cycling circuits were timed, my push-ups and sit-ups had to reach a minimum count, but together, we made it through these four physically excruciating weeks. The weight loss soon began to reflect on my face as my jawline and cheekbones sharpened. Even Papaji's weight loss was visible in his loosening uniform. Then the day of the appeal medical board came, and Papaji and I left for Delhi. Maa and Papaji always inculcated in Dada and me a sense of responsibility by sending us everywhere all by ourselves, even when I had left for the hostel. But Papaji decided to accompany me this time.

As much as he tried to hide his nervousness, I could see it on his face. I was equally nervous. Upon reaching Delhi, we reported to the AFCME, where, after the initial documentation, I was sent for a weight check.

I had lost eight kilos. I had crossed my first obstacle. But uncertainty still loomed over the second, bigger obstacle—the anthropometry tests. A doctor carefully took various measurements of my body. I could feel beads of sweat break out on my forehead. My height had not changed and I had resigned myself to the fact that I might have to spend the rest of my service years delivering ground-staff duties only. The doctor asked Papaji and me to sit in the waiting room. As we waited, Papaji tried to divert my attention by talking about random subjects, but I only nodded absentmindedly. After half an hour, I was finally called to the commandant's office.

'May I come in, Sir?' I asked.

'Please,' replied the commandant, an air force officer who sat behind a big walnut-wood table dressed in his decorated uniform. 'Have a seat.' He took off his cap and continued. 'So the good news for you is that the board has cleared your TR for weight. Well done.'

'Thank you, Sir,' I replied.

'But you're one centimetre short of the minimum height required for flying.' My face drooped and I stared at the floor.

'However,' he continued, and I listened without looking up, 'as per the anthropometry tests, your arm reach and leg length have been found to be one centimetre more than the minimum required.' At this, I looked up at him.

'And so I have decided to waive off the one centimetre and recommend you for flying.'

I could not believe my ears. What had just happened?

'I think you were born to be a pilot,' he said, and continued to give me further directions on the documentation and more. But a strange silence had fallen over me. When I came out of his office, there was a wide smile on my face. Papaji immediately understood what must have happened. I ran to hug him.

'You did it, Papaji,' I exclaimed.

'We did it,' he replied. 'Now let's go to the cafeteria. I've ordered something for us to celebrate.'

'What?' I asked.

'Cassata,' he replied.

NINE

15 January 1995

The reception we, the new cadets, received at the Air Force Academy (AFA) in Dundigal was a very cold one, far from anything I had imagined. There were no welcome signs, no cheers, nothing at all. There was only the customary silence of a disciplined life, akin to any other cantonment. The academy—located twenty-five kilometres from the twin cities of Hyderabad and Secunderabad—had been established in 1971 to train to the flying, technical and ground-duty branches, as well as officers of the army and navy. Every year, two batches of pilots graduate from the academy to proceed for further training in the fighter, transport and helicopter wings at other training establishments. When I entered the academy with my luggage, I found myself staring at the numerous vintage aircraft on display at various locations inside the academy. 'Achievement through diligence', the academy's motto, was inscribed in many places. I walked past all four squadrons of the academy to reach the flight cadets' mess (FCM), wondering whether I'd spend my training time in the Aquino, Brar, Chitnis or Katre squadrons. When I stood in front of the FCM, which stood calmly in the middle of seven thousand acres of the academy, I couldn't help but imagine how many cadets would have started their journey right from where I was standing. We were all dressed in civvies and stood in small groups, wondering what would happen next, until a photographer arrived and asked us to line up so he could click a photograph. As soon as he had finished, an instructor of the rank of wing commander arrived, along with a bunch of aircraftmen. A very short, crisp introductory speech was delivered by him, followed by certain instructions on general dos and don'ts. Squadrons and academy numbers were allotted to each cadet, soon after the aircraftmen finished checking everyone's luggage to ensure nobody was carrying unauthorized items such as eatables, medicines or cameras. I was allotted to the Brar Squadron and my academy number was 182860.

'You may all go to your squadrons now, keep your luggage, change into whites and come back to fall in at this same place in thirty minutes. Your time here starts now, so does your training,' he said with an air of command. But he was clearly not impressed with the lethargic reaction of everyone present, as they slowly turned around and walked towards the squadrons. He shouted, 'Did you not listen when I said you weren't authorized to walk? You are first-termers and you should be seen doubling up . . . always. Starting from NOW!'

All of a sudden, every girl was on the double, including me. The realization that training had already begun was overwhelming. Running with the luggage took a toll on me and I started to pant. Little did I know I'd be running with more weight on my back very soon. I landed up outside Brar Squadron, along with five other female cadets, helping each other get our luggage to the first floor. My room was second from the last on the right flank. This was when I realized I was on my own from now. The thought was quite frightening. I did not know if I was even prepared to face what was about to come my way.

'Do you have an extra white shirt?' a girl asked as she peeped through the half-open door of my cabin while I was hurriedly unpacking.

'Yes, I think I do.' I took out a shirt and turned to look at the girl. She looked bigger and taller than me. 'But . . . I don't think this will fit you,' I added.

'It's okay. I'll manage,' she said with a smile as she took the shirt from me hurriedly.

'Oh, I'm Anuradha,' she said before leaving.

'I'm Gunjan . . .' I replied as she disappeared from sight.

The fall-in took place half an hour later, at the cycle stand in front of the FCM. All of us lined up in attention as the instructor addressed us again. Certain rules pertaining to the academy were relayed to us. 'You shouldn't be seen walking, you should wish your seniors, no matter where you are and how many times you see them, you should learn and follow mess etiquette, you should do whatever your seniors ask you to, be at the right place, at the right time and in the right rig . . .' and so on. With each instruction, the seriousness of the training dawned on all of us. We dispersed for lunch after the address was over. There was an awkward silence all around. After another half hour we were supposed to fall in at the training ground for evening games practice in the games rig.

'Are they always going to keep us this busy?' Anuradha asked from behind as she tried to catch up with me as I made my way to the dining table.

'I guess,' I replied. 'My father tells me that every minute inside the academy is calculated. The training never stops.'

'I don't mind as long as they give us good food,' she commented as we lined up with our plates in front of the serving counters.

'I don't mind as long as I get enough sleep,' I said. But I knew I had wished for too much. If there was one thing I was going to be deprived of, it was sleep. Eighteen months of training is not just five hundred and forty days of training, but five hundred and forty nights too. I would learn this soon enough.

The games period started with a three-kilometre run in the squads, where each squad was headed by a physical-training instructor aircraftman. It was followed by intense PT. No games were played that day. After about an hour, we retired to our squadrons, panting and dripping in sweat. 'This, too, shall pass,' I said to myself. No sooner had we taken a bath than we were called for a squadron fall-in. The senior-term cadets were waiting for us downstairs as we lined up in the central hall. We somehow knew we were in for some trouble. One of us had forgotten to wish a senior-termer earlier during the day, and since the academy was about 'all for one, one for all', all of us were called for a punishment parade. Introductions began with us—the first-termers—in high-plank position. Some of us couldn't even remain in the position for thirty seconds. Whenever one of us fell flat on the floor, the others were asked by the seniors to do more push-ups. Punishments in the academy were commonly known as 'ragda'. And we were undergoing our first ragda on our first day. This was just one of the numerous punishments the seniors would give us until we became seniors the following term ourselves. And that's when we would do the same to our juniors. Thus, the cycle would go on.

'Why is your hair not in place?' asked a senior flight cadet, Sonia, as I struggled to keep myself in the plank position. I did not know how to respond and stayed quiet.

'I'm asking you,' she bent forward and said.

'I . . . I tried my best, Ma'am,' I said, stuttering. I had applied enough oil and had tied my hair into a tight bun, so why was I being checked? She pulled a strand out of my bun and asked, 'Is this your best?' And then she shouted loudly into my ear, 'It's not TIGHT ENOUGH!' I flinched. 'And you have the guts to answer back?' she shouted angrily. 'Get up, you lazy fools. Run to your cabins and get your oil bottles. We'll teach you how to make a bun.'

And this is how I was introduced to my first 'oil parade' in the academy. It was one of the most common punishments, in which the flight cadets were made to oil their hair until oil dripped on their foreheads and faces. Some other punishments, included drinking mugs of water from a half-filled bucket and then spinning around until they threw up, only to roll around in each other's vomit— front rolls, back rolls, crawling, legs up against the wall and anything else that could be physically and mentally excruciating. As first-termers, we were most prone to making small mistakes and so, punishments were given all through the day and the night. This included both official punishments by instructors and unofficial punishments by seniors. There was no time for rest and respite. Strict discipline was ensured, and rules were taught with an iron hand. There was no room for even the slightest error, during training as well as in battle.

After only a day, the tiredness reflected on our drooping faces. I could feel every muscle in my body turning sore. The skin on my back burnt as sweat rolled down the cuts and bruises from having continuously rolled on gravel. As I took a shower in the evening, right before the open-door study period, I convinced myself to shut my mind and stop worrying—it was the only way I would make it through the academy. Open-door study period was observed for an hour every evening, from seven to eight. The juniors would sit and study, and one senior would be on watch. If anybody was found sleeping, the entire batch of first-termers would get punished after dinner. And after a day's backbreaking training, sleep was unavoidable. So were the late-night punishments. Somehow, I made it through the study period and went for dinner with Anuradha. Each first-termer was made to sit next to a senior-term flight cadet, and it was the senior's responsibility to teach mess etiquette to the first-termer. The teaching inside the mess would go on for only a week. Punishments would follow later, if mistakes still persisted. A-first term cadet would generally be so lost trying to catch up with the tight schedule that mistakes would be unavoidable. It is rightly said that punishments lay eggs. One punishment always leads to another and so on.

Dinner inside the FCM was well-cooked, balanced and delicious. It was followed by mouth-watering pudding. Tired as we were, we were all famished and ate like horses. Luckily, we were allowed to sleep at nine, which was the official 'lights-off' time. While I was preparing my dress for the next day, I started to miss home. To avoid homesickness, I thought of going to Anuradha's cabin next to mine. She wasn't asleep either. When I entered her cabin, she was struggling to put her towel on the window to cover it. Curtains were not yet issued to the cadets due to some logistical delay and we had had to think of makeshift arrangements.

'They expect us to undergo ragda but can't even provide curtains on time,' I commented as I helped Anuradha.

'Must have been an administrative officer's laziness,' she said.

'Must have been the commandant's fault too,' I added. 'After all, he's responsible for the well-being of the academy's pupils. A careless commandant is the last thing this academy needs.'

'The commandant has other things to look after too,' she said in a tone that sounded defensive.

'You sound as if you know the commandant,' I commented as we finished covering the window.

'Well,' she took a pause, picked up a glass of water and said, 'I think I do.'

'Yes, and I think I know the president of India,' I said comically.

She smiled at me and said, 'I'm the commandant's daughter, Gunjan.'

I let out a laugh at first, but then I stared at Anuradha and knew she wasn't lying.

'I'm Anuradha Nair, Air Marshal K.N. Nair's daughter,' she said plainly. 'But please don't tell anyone.'

'Oh, I'm sorry if I said anything bad,' I said.

'It's okay,' she said.

Being the commandant's daughter must have had its own privileges, I thought at first. But Anuradha was just another cadet and liked being treated as one, I would realize later. For instance, the mess secretary had offered Anuradha curtains on the first day, but she had refused, saying she would take them once they had been issued for all other cadets. Her parents lived inside the academy, and yet, they would never come to meet her until she would earn her liberty. This, and many other similar instances, spoke a lot about what kind of person she was, and that somehow drew me to her. We would become inseparable friends during the entire training and would remain friends long after it ended.

I tasked Anuradha with waking me up the next morning. I had never been a morning person, and for someone who could sleep through a bomb blast, I knew I'd miss out on every alarm. She did as I had asked; little did she know that she would have to carry out this duty for the next three terms. The central fall-in in the games rig outside the FCM was scheduled at quarter to six in the morning. A report was given to the instructor officer sharp at six. Taking reports has always been a mandatory routine task before and after any kind of fall-in or parade, to account for missing persons or persons employed elsewhere. There's a disciplined procedure of its own that all of us would be taught in due time. After the report was over, the PT ustads of the respective squadrons took their squads for a three-kilometre run, followed by a back-breaking session of physical training. Exhausted from forty-five minutes of PT parade, we wolfed down our breakfast, went to our cabins for a quick shower and gathered outside the FCM again for another central fall-in. The entire day's schedule was then announced to us. Bicycles were issued in the administrative block. 'Take care of your bicycles better than your boyfriends' is what was commonly said, and, quite truly, these bicycles would be our only mode of conveyance and any malfunction of it would mean being late and, ultimately, more punishments. Each bicycle was allotted a number for identification. The next thing on the schedule was the issue of various uniforms and overalls that we would require during training. We were dispersed for lunch after an address by the chief instructor, in which we were told the detailed schedule for the next six months.

There was a different schedule for cadets who had qualified for flying and those who had qualified for technical or administrative duties. Flying cadets would undergo a mechanical conversion flight course on an HPT-32 fixed wing aircraft for four weeks, before they were allowed to even go near an actual aircraft. They would be taught the basics of flying, including engine, airframe and everything technical related to the flying of an aircraft. They would be made to appear for an exam after that, and only those who would pass would be taught to fly. All this while, the daily schedule would remain unchanged. The day would start with a rigorous PT or drill parade, followed by classes until we broke for lunch. Preparation of upcoming sports events would continue during the games parade. Open-door study period would be observed religiously, followed by dinner and the usual ragda session until midnight or, at times, even till first light.

Four weeks passed without me realizing that the exam had edged closer; I had wasted most of my free time compensating for my lack of sleep. But then I had Anuradha to motivate me and teach me everything that I had missed. Both of us had lost a lot of weight in those four weeks. Our skin tone had darkened, and our cheekbones and jawlines would shine on a bright sunny day. It was the same with every cadet. I wondered if my own parents would recognize me. I had not spoken to them in a while and missed them a lot. I didn't even get enough time to write to them frequently. After the initial few troublesome days, I had finally adjusted myself to the academy's way of life in those four weeks. But waking up in the early morning was still a pain for me and I would often look at the stars and ask, 'Why did I come here?' But the airplanes soaring against the dark blue sky would remind me of my purpose. Yet, there was one thing that stood between me and my dream of flying—the exam. And even until the morning of the exam, I wondered if I was fully prepared. But whether I would fly or not, only the results would tell.

TEN

'I don't think I'll pass,' I said to Anuradha, panicking.

'You definitely won't if you keep whining like this,' Anuradha said as she passed the book to me. 'Now revise quickly.'

'I don't know what to focus on,' I lamented as I turned the pages of the book. 'Safety procedures or technical data? Only four hours are left for the exam!'

'There's barely any time! Just go through what you can,' Anuradha advised as she walked out of the room.

The first light of the sun lit up the night sky as I sat there wondering what to do. Anuradha had done her best to make me understand most of the concepts, but to be able to write, I had to memorize the language of the book. The scope of the syllabus was so wide that I knew I wouldn't be able to read everything in just four hours. So I had to be selective, I had to follow my instincts. Honestly, my instincts, too, had given up on me at that time. It added to my frustration and I threw the book away. I wished Papaji was there to help me.

* * *

April 1987

Tenth standard had been one of my best in school. I had made some of my most wonderful friends in that class. It was an age when friends mattered more than family. Our old-fashioned bungalow in Babina, Uttar Pradesh, where Papaji had been posted, would mostly be bustling with my friends coming and leaving every now and then. This would keep Maa busy in the kitchen as she would try to tend to the demands of each friend. The only respite for her were on Thursdays and Saturdays, when my friends and I would go to watch movies at an auditorium inside the cantonment. My scooter-riding lessons also began in the tenth standard. Papaji would take me out on his scooter after dinner every day, since the roads inside the cantonment would generally be empty then. But there came a time when I started making excuses to avoid learning how to ride the scooter.

My friend, Navneet, had told me that I had ruined my hair by wearing the helmet every day and the other girls had started noticing it too. It wasn't as fluffy as before, I was told. So I refrained from going with Papaji after a few days. But he wouldn't listen. At times he would take me for these riding lessons against my will. This business of learning how to ride a scooter wasn't left unfinished. Consequently, I got my learner's licence. The bright side was that I could go out on the scooter with my friends. But I would take the helmet off after I would be out of Papaji's watchful gaze. The hair was a priority at that age, more than safety. Papaji's instructions to always wear a helmet were ignored.

One fine Sunday in April, Navneet and I decided to drive to Sukma Dukma Dam, which was also a famous tourist destination. It was a breezy day and staying indoors would have been a crime. I called her to my place. Maa packed us some sandwiches and pakoras that we could enjoy on the reservoir's shores. We were set to leave by eleven.

'Don't forget the helmets . . . one for the pillion rider too,' Papaji reminded us as he heard me kick-start the scooter. He was sitting in the lawn with his face buried in a newspaper.

'Sure, Papaji,' I replied as I passed the helmet to Navneet, who shook her head in disapproval. 'Only until we get out of here,' I whispered to Navneet, and she took the helmet reluctantly.

Papaji lowered his newspaper to check if we were wearing the helmets as instructed. Seeing that we had complied, he smiled and wished us goodbye as we sped out of the bungalow on the scooter. No sooner had we moved a few hundred metres away from home than we removed our helmets. Soon, we were flying down the road at a speed that could rival a cheetah's. It was thrilling. I could feel the wind in my hair, and it made me happy, so much so that I forgot to slow down as we entered the main road. Just as I steered left, a cyclist appeared out of nowhere in front of me, and I panicked. It was too late to apply the brakes and I collided with the cyclist head-on. The next thing I remember was lying flat on the road with pedestrians gathered around me, helping me up. I felt a sharp pain on my right cheekbone as I tried to get up. Navneet was lying next to me, trying to get up too. Another group of men pulled the half-conscious cyclist from under my scooter. He was seemingly unhurt. Blood was dripping down my chin. Luckily, Navneet had got only a few minor bruises. I looked at my reflection in the rear-view mirror of my fallen scooter. My right cheek had turned a dark red.

I knew I was in for some serious trouble. Papaji would know I wasn't wearing a helmet if he saw me. The bleeding stopped but I feared going back home. So I dropped Navneet off at her house and headed back, praying for some miracle to avoid confronting Papaji. As I edged closer to my home, I thought of sneaking in by quietly pulling the scooter inside. I peered over the boundary wall to see if Papaji was still in the lawn. There was nobody, save a chair and a small peg table. So I quickly went inside and parked the scooter in the stand.

'How bad is it?' It was Papaji's voice from behind me. I stopped dead in my tracks.

'What, Papaji?' I was terrified.

'I can see the dents on the scooter,' he said plainly.

'Oh . . . it's just a small dent. I'll get it fixed.' I trembled as I spoke.

'It's not about the scooter, Gunju,' he said. 'How bad is your injury?'

I did not say anything.

'Turn around,' he said calmly.

Knowing that there was no escape, I slowly turned to face him, with my gaze fixed on the ground. The muscles of his face twitched as he saw my bruised cheek. He lifted my face, turned it slightly to the left for a better look at the injury.

'If only you had listened to me and kept the helmet on,' he spoke softly.

Tears of repentance filled my eyes. 'I'm sorry, Papaji,' I finally broke into tears. 'I was wrong. I'm sorry. I should have listened to you. It hurts really badly.'

Papaji said nothing and hugged me. He took me inside, cleaned my wound and applied an antiseptic, poured me a glass of hot turmeric milk and sat beside me. The only thing I still remember him saying is this—*Before you learn to do something, learn all the ways to not do it. Remember, safety is paramount.*

* * *

The sudden memory of this incident sparked my instincts and I felt like I knew what I had to focus on: safety procedures and safety checklist. The exam was scheduled to start at ten in the morning. The cadets were supposed to be seated at half past nine. Question papers were distributed ten minutes prior, as everyone sat anxiously in wait. When the examiner approached my seat with the question papers, I immediately started to go through the questions. To my surprise and relief, a major chunk of the question paper was on the topic I had thoroughly prepared for—safety procedures. I scribbled on the answer sheet continuously throughout the two hours of the exam. It was over sooner than I had expected, and I was pretty pleased with my performance. I looked at Anuradha, who was seated in another corner of the examination hall. Seeing her signature cheerful smile, I knew the exam had gone well for her too. Results were announced two days after the exam and all the flight cadets had passed.

Now that we had qualified to fly, the allotment of squadrons for flight cadets was the first thing on the schedule. There were four squadrons, numbered from one to four. I was allotted Squadron Number 2. Five to six cadets from each squadron were allotted an instructor who would be responsible for their flying training. The schedule for the next five months until we would clear the solo flying test was also conveyed to us. Then onwards, two squadrons would undergo morning flying and the other two afternoon flying, on alternate weeks. Though both the sessions were equally hard, I particularly disliked the morning sessions. Every flying session started with a central briefing, known as a 'mass briefing', which would be scheduled at five in the morning. Flight cadets were supposed to be seated in the briefing room by half past four. This meant waking up at half past three in the morning, and for someone like me, who loved to sleep, I despised morning sessions more than anything else. Every mass briefing started with a time check to ensure everyone's time was synchronized. It would be followed by a briefing by the meteorological officer, who would tell us about the weather conditions during the upcoming flying hours. An air traffic control officer would then brief us on NOTAMS (a special notification issued to pilots before a flight, advising them on the circumstances related to the state of flying), outstation traffic at the base and other available facilities for the day. This would be followed by the technical officer's briefing and, lastly, a 'pilot order', which would be read by one of the trainee cadets. After the mass briefing, we would be sent to our respective squadrons to change from our usual light-blue shirt and blue-grey trousers to flying overalls, flying shoes and gloves. During the initial week of flying training, I had to manage with an oversized overall, since there was no size available that could fit me as I was the shortest among the cadets. Anuradha would make fun of me in the oversized overalls. I took the teasing sportingly. Together, we would go to the cafeteria of our squadron to grab a quick bite of a sandwich and sometimes a bowl of porridge. Eating a light breakfast before flights was mandatory. Each cadet would then go to their respective squadron's ops room, where a white board with instructions would be kept for them to read through. Details regarding which cadet would undergo which sortie* and at what time would generally be inscribed on the board. I remember a quote that our instructor would always write on the white board: 'You need to be 200 per cent prepared on the ground to be able to perform 100 per cent in air. And remember, you must always think ahead of your aircraft.'

---

* A sortie is when a group of soldiers is sent on a specific mission. A fighter pilot's sortie might involve a mission to drop a bomb on a target and return to base. Even a practice flight is called a sortie in air force parlance.

Once this was done, the cadets would report to their respective instructors to tell them that they were ready for the sortie. The instructor would then quiz the cadets to check how prepared they were for it. Once satisfied, the instructor and the cadet would go to the daily servicing section, where the technical staff would make the instructor sign an aircraft maintenance form, Form 700, containing the entire technical and service history of the aircraft, after all the necessary technical checks were carried out.

What followed was one of my favourite things during the entire training. The pupil and the instructor would walk to the aircraft together. It would be a meticulously disciplined walk, where the instructor would walk on the right and the pupil on the left, a step behind the instructor. Together, they would walk in step towards the aircraft, their helmets in their left hands, resting against the waist. A sense of pride filled my heart every time I did it. Even to this day, it makes my hair stand on end when I think about it.

Certain external visual checks to ensure that the covers were on or the chokes in place would be carried out while approaching the aircraft. Both the instructor and the pupil would then place their helmets on one of the wings and go around the aircraft, carefully performing mandatory checks as per the checklist. The checklist was meant to be learnt by heart, and included a plethora of procedures before start-up, after start-up and even when airborne.

I remember the first time I entered the aircraft with my instructor—a sense of achievement and pride engulfed my heart and mind. I imagined Papaji standing at the edge of the tarmac, looking at me with a broad smile. I imagined Dada shouting loudly, 'Way to go, Gunju!' I imagined Maa standing next to Papaji, telling him how proud she was to see me preparing for take-off. I desperately wished for my entire family to be there to see me fly for the first time. But I was still happy knowing that I had achieved what I had set out to, and it was only a matter of time until I earned the ranks. I was happy that Papaji would soon brag about his daughter to his course mates. I was happy that Maa would finally see the disciplined soldier inside her mischievous daughter.

As my aircraft left the tarmac, I saw myself advancing towards a new horizon where the most important purpose of my life awaited. But the path was still laid with back-breaking obstacles, tests so challenging they would go beyond my limits. All I needed to do was remain resilient. All that any cadet needs in the academy is to keep doing everything they are asked to—without giving much thought to it. The military is not the place for those who apply logic to orders; the military is for those who know how to follow orders in letter and spirit. Because when in war, logic induces fear and fear induces cowardice. But those who are only trained to follow orders fail to recognize fear. Those who follow orders are the ones who make a difference. And this entire process begins in the academy itself. So when I flew my first sortie, I realized this was exactly what I needed to do, and I promised myself I would keep going and face whatever came my way. The flying training had just begun. The first aim was to qualify for a solo flight. I could not wait to achieve this aim, little knowing then that this would put me in a situation I would never have wished for.

ELEVEN

'Good evening, Ma'am. Flight Cadet Gunjan Saxena reporting for lights-out parade state,' I said after knocking on the cabin door exactly twice, as per the instructions of Preeti Lavale, the woman under officer (WUO). A WUO is an appointment given to one senior-term cadet of each squadron; they generally hold the responsibility of grooming the junior cadets for correct military bearing and for all things related to training. A cadet from flank* had to report to the WUO sharp at ten in the night for the

---

* A flank is generally a 'side', for example, the left flank or the right flank of a column. In a barracks, a flank is a side, either left or right. Here, it means the rooms on one side of one floor in a building.

lights-out report, which had to be prepared in a particular format. I was chosen to do it for my flank.

'I can't hear you,' WUO Preeti Lavale said coldly from across the closed door even though I had been loud enough. 'Be louder.'

I repeated the same line a little louder than the last.

'I still can't hear you,' she replied. I screamed at the top of my voice this time.

'Bend,' she said as she opened the door and stood cross-armed against the side-jambs. Not knowing what I could have done wrong, I returned a questioning look. 'You want to disobey, you tiny first-termer?' she said angrily. 'Bend!' To bend always meant to get into a high-plank position, and I did as was asked. There was no way I could question her. Nobody questions a senior in the academy. 'Next time make sure you are loud in your first attempt itself,' she said plainly. 'Now get up.'

After reading the report I had shared with her on a piece of paper, she looked at me with disappointment on her face. 'Start rolling,' she commanded. I started front-rolling on the floor, but I was quite sure I hadn't made any mistakes in finalizing the report that night. It had been more than ten days that I had started reporting to the WUO, and even though I tried my best to not disappoint her, I ended up making one mistake or another. Sometimes I would get punished for writing the report in a wrong format or for leaving an error in the report or for showing up outside her cabin two minutes early or late. Then there were times when I would simply doze off while making the report and not show up at all. My fellow cadets had started joking that the floor outside the WUO's cabin always shone 'from Gunjan's rolling'. But that night, I was sure there was no mistake. After about fifteen minutes of rolling and push-ups, the WUO sent me to my cabin after saying that she did not like my handwriting and that I should improve it. It was just another night in the life of a flight cadet!

We were halfway through the first term when the eighth check sortie knocked on our doors. During flying training, there are certain check sorties scheduled at different stages to scrutinize the progress of a cadet before they impart further training. This was one such check sortie, which we were supposed to fly with the chief flying instructor (CFI). Anuradha, Supreet and I were trained by one of the best instructors in the academy, Sqn Ldr S.K. Borbora, a short-built, generous, round-faced Assamese officer. But when it came to flying with the CFI Wing Commander S.S. Patil, even the best trainees broke out into cold sweat. Though professional and energetic, Wing Commander Patil was also known among the cadets for blowing his top inside the cockpit if someone failed to perform well. If being short-tempered wasn't all, his austerity was exemplary. Getting into his bad books had often led to cadets getting demoted or even thrown out of the flying branch altogether. The CFI always demanded meticulous performances from cadets to achieve certain benchmarks in the flying training under his command. When the day of my eighth check sortie came, I was quite sure I'd end up disappointing the CFI, just as I always disappointed my squadron's WUO. Little did I know then that the WUO's strict attitude towards me would lead me to finally focus on minute details. It could have been one reason that my check sortie went well with the CFI, who seemed quite impressed after the sortie was over. In fact, he was so impressed that he asked my instructor, 'Babs Sir' as we called him, to prepare me for a solo sortie after my tenth sortie, where I would have to fly the aircraft from take-off to landing all on my own. Generally, it was the fourteenth sortie where a solo check would be carried out. To go solo after just the tenth sortie would be quite early for me and I could get worked up, Babs Sir knew this well. So he kept this news from me. It was during the debriefing of my ninth sortie that Babs Sir broke the news to me that I would be going solo the next day, right after my tenth sortie.

'But how is this possible, Sir?' I started to whine. 'I'm not even prepared for it. It should be done after my fourteenth. Why now?'

'Don't get nervous, Gunjan, just fly a normal sortie. Fly how you fly with me. If you won't perform well, he won't clear you. It'll be recorded as a normal training sortie then,' Babs Sir tried to reassure me. He and I both knew that if it didn't go well, there were chances the CFI would put it in my folder as a failed check sortie. If a cadet didn't clear a check sortie and it got recorded in his or her folder, he or she might have to go through a termination review board and be thrown out of the flying branch eventually.

'Don't worry, nothing bad will happen,' Babs Sir said, and asked me to go and get a good night's sleep. Anuradha tried to cheer me up as we pedalled our bicycles towards our squadron. I should focus on the bright side of it, she said. But I was too nervous to even listen to her. After the open-door study period and a quick dinner, I came back to my cabin to prepare the lights-out report. To my astonishment, WUO Preeti Lavale called me to her cabin at nine instead of ten. When she began my ragda session, even after I had requested her to excuse me for the night, it added to my frustration. A rigorous half-hour of punishment followed. When I finally reached my cabin by half past nine, I was too exhausted to worry about the next day. No sooner did I hit the bed than I fell into a dreamless slumber. Anuradha would tell me later that the WUO had intentionally planned the punishment session so I would be exhausted and fall asleep, instead of staying awake and worrying about the check sortie.

I woke up the next day even before Anuradha's alarm went off. When she came to my cabin, I was already getting ready. 'When you sit inside the cockpit, just imagine you are alone,' she advised. She was equally worried. It was one of those rare occasions that I was seated before time for the mass briefing. But I do not remember listening to any of it that day. I desperately wanted Babs Sir to do something and postpone the sortie. But he seemed confident about me and assured me in the ops room that it would all go well. We went for a half-hour sortie together, in which he made me revise all the basics and aerobatic manoeuvres. When we returned, I could see the CFI already standing at the tarmac in his overalls, with a ready aircraft. As soon as we landed, the CFI took me with him without even letting me talk to Babs Sir. I was so scared I wanted to cry. But it was too late. The solo check sortie had begun. Before I could say anything, I had already taken off.

To clear a solo check, one must show the CFI three consecutive safe landings, apart from a plethora of other checks, since landing is always the most difficult part. It was a bright sunny day and the sky was placidly clear, one of the most perfect days for flying. What wasn't perfect was the man I accompanied in this sortie. His presence alone made me so nervous that I committed some really silly mistakes during the first landing, mistakes I had never committed earlier with Babs Sir. Wing Commander Patil blew his top inside the cockpit.

'What the hell was that? You've come for a solo check, do you realize that? This is what you want to show me?'

Since it was a roller take-off, I opened the throttle again after touch-down, going for a take-off right after landing without stopping, and advanced high into the blue sky. The CFI was shouting so loud I couldn't even hear the engine revving. 'If you repeat this in the next landing, I'll throw you out of the flying branch,' he shouted one last time before he went quiet again. My hands shivered and tears filled my eyes. I had to do something. I could not afford to lose my calm at this moment. I closed my eyes and ignored all the sounds that were reaching my ears. Everything went dark and blank for a moment.

* * *

June 1987

Summers in Babina were unforgiving. Papaji would take Dada and me to the swimming pool in the officers' mess in the late afternoons almost every day to deal with the scorching heat. Dada was a good swimmer and would use this opportunity to brush up on his swimming skills, whereas I would simply while away time in frivolous activities. But Papaji had a different plan for us. He had put in our names for a swimming competition scheduled at the end of the month without letting us know. He would only tell us four days prior. While it excited Dada, I was left disappointed, since I knew I would lose. Other girls of the society knew how to dive, but even though I was a good swimmer, I only knew how to jump and not dive. So Papaji started to teach me how to dive. But days passed and I still could not learn.

'I won't be able to accompany you tomorrow,' Papaji said to us after he hung up the phone and came to the dining table. The swimming competition was scheduled for the next day.

'It's good you won't have to see Gunjan fail,' Dada commented. Papaji stared at Dada angrily.

'I will not fail,' I retorted.

'Why do you think Gunjan will fail?' Papaji asked.

'She doesn't know how to dive,' Dada said. 'Others will take the lead by diving.'

'So what if she doesn't know how to dive? She will win,' Maa barged in, siding with me.

'If you want your daughter to win, tell her to dive. Even if it'll be a bad dive, it will still be better than a jump,' Dada said to Maa. He clearly didn't want me to jump. I knew his friends would make fun of him if I jumped instead of diving. That's how boys were.

'I will ask the referee to allow Gunjan to start from inside the pool,' Maa said.

'No,' Dada and I said in unison. 'You won't do any such thing.'

Just like any other teenager, I did not want my parents to stand up for me.

'Whatever you do, just give it your best shot,' Papaji said, putting an end to the conversation.

The officers' mess inside the Babina cantonment was readied according to the ceremonial layout. Flags were placed at the entrance and a red carpet was laid down; it went up till the chief guest's chair. Two lancers, dressed in the Sikh regimental outfit, stood guard at the main door to welcome the chief guest, who was the station commander's wife. The competition was scheduled to begin at ten in the morning. Officers, their wives and children, including participants, started trickling in almost an hour earlier. Maa accompanied me and Dada and wished us luck before she went to her seat in the audience section. The referee whistled for the lifeguards to take their positions. The timekeepers occupied their seats as Dada and I walked towards the changing room. I was to go first.

'Remember, just dive,' Dada held me by my shoulders and firmly said. I nodded and went to the changing room. The chief guest arrived at quarter to ten. The first round was to be held among women under eighteen. We lined up at our respective starting points at the edge of the swimming pool. I looked around, to my left and right, and saw my competitors prepare for a dive. I could feel butterflies in my stomach. For a moment, it felt like the entire crowd was looking only at me. It added to my nervousness. People would laugh at me if I jumped instead of dived, I thought. My gaze found Dada's, standing at the other end of the pool with his friends, nodding slightly to remind me that I should not jump. The referee then asked us to take the final position. I could see Dada turn his back towards me and cover his eyes with his hands. The referee blew the whistle and even though I tried to dive, I ended up jumping into the pool while every other competitor floated ahead of me after their successful dives. For a moment, I struggled to pace up. It was a moment of realization and I understood I was going to fail. But something inside me was just not ready to give up yet. So I closed my eyes and ignored all the cheers and other sounds, and moved my arms and legs as fast as I could. Every bit of my energy went into pushing me ahead under the water's surface. Not even once did I raise my mouth out of the water to breathe until my hands finally felt the touch of marble, and it was then that I realized that I had reached the opposite side of the pool. The cheering reached my ears as I came out of the water, breathing heavily. After I wiped my eyes, I looked to my left and right and found that I was alone at the finishing point and the other candidates were still behind me. It had to be some kind of error, I thought at first. But when I saw Dada's friends making him turn around, pointing in my direction with a cheerful smile, I realized that I had won. Dada punched the air and jumped in excitement. Even though my start had been bad, I had managed to succeed, and it had been possible only because I had not lost my calm. Life had taught me what 'do or die' actually meant. I was going to lose, so I thought of doing so with dignity and channelled all my energy into my arms and legs. Instead of giving up, I ended up seizing the day. Papaji, Maa and Dada were so proud of me that day. I made it a point to remind myself of this incident if I was ever faced with such a situation again.

* * *

When I opened my eyes, I took a deep breath and turned my aircraft back for another landing. Only this time, I did not let the CFI bother me with his shouting. To me, he did not even exist inside the aircraft in that moment. I only did what I had learnt from Babs Sir. The next two landings went well, without any hitches. As I taxied my aircraft on the tarmac after the check sortie was over, I could see Babs Sir, Anuradha and Supreet standing near the hangar. Whenever a cadet goes for their first solo flight, whether they have cleared it is denoted by the aircraft being turned off or not. If a cadet clears the solo, the aircraft will not be turned off; only the CFI will get out of the cockpit and the cadet will need to turn back and go for a solo flight. Babs Sir stood there, biting his nails, waiting to see whether my aircraft would turn off or not. When the aircraft came to a standstill, the canopy opened and the CFI crawled out, signalling to me to turn around and go back for a solo flight. I looked at Babs Sir, who gave me a thumbs up. I blinked away tears of joy and went for the first solo flight of my career. Even though the start was bumpy, I had cleared my solo check, becoming the first in my course to go solo. When I approached for landing, I saw Babs Sir standing against the ACP hut* at the start of the runway. He was smiling. I was smiling too. I taxied my aircraft back to the hangar and ran straight to Babs Sir to tell him everything in detail.

'Your sortie is not over until you sign,' Babs Sir reminded me, so I turned back and ran towards the hangar. In all the excitement, I had forgotten to sign off on Form 700. Before I could go back to Babs Sir, the CFI called me to his office for a debriefing. After this I ran straight to Babs Sir and told him everything that

---

* An ACP, or an approach control pilot, hut is a small hut at the end of the runway to assist trainee pilots in landing. They are in direct RT contact with the pilot.

had happened in a single breath. Anuradha and Supreet listened intently.

'I knew you would do it. You've made me proud,' Babs Sir said.

Anuradha and Supreet congratulated me. The next thing I did was call my parents from the STD phone in our squadron's cafeteria. They couldn't believe what I told them.

'Did you fly alone?' Papaji asked.

'Did you take the aircraft into the sky all by yourself?' Maa asked excitedly.

'How many birds did you hit?' Dada joked. My family was very happy and proud. And I was happy that they were happy. That was what I had always wanted to do.

The first term's flying training was over for me before any other cadet had cleared it. Another good thing was that I had been granted liberty during the weekends to go out into the city—part of the privilege I had earned after clearing my solo. But I preferred to spend it at Anuradha's house, savouring home-cooked food and talking endlessly with her and her mother. The bad side of clearing the solo first, however, was that I had been assigned to Wing Commander Patil as his pupil. It meant that I could no longer fly with Babs Sir. But it was all for my good, Babs Sir had convinced me. He would always tell me to focus on the next two terms, which would form the basis of my actual military service.

The first term drew to an end. Every year, a team of pilots from the Aircrew Examination Board (AEB) visited various flying stations to assess pilots and categorize them. A team of pilots from AEB was scheduled to visit the Air Force Academy Dundigal in May 1995. The entire academy—from the directing to the administrative staff—could be seen gearing up for this visit. The instructor pilots, too, could be seen flying practice sorties, since the AEB team would fly with the instructors. One cadet from each term would be chosen to fly with the AEB pilots. Usually, male cadets would get this opportunity, as it had only been over a year that women had started flying in the Indian Air Force. It never occurred to me in my wildest dreams that I would be made to fly a sortie with the AEB pilots. Two days before the sorties with the AEB were planned, the CFI called me to his office.

'The CO of AEB, Group Captain R. Damodaran, is going to fly a sortie with you after two days. Now gear up and give him a good show.'

His words left me stunned for a moment, but then I managed a 'yes, Sir'. I broke this news to Anuradha and Supreet in the changing room. Both were very happy and wished me luck. But I was scared, since I had had a long break from flying after clearing solo. Others probably overheard our conversation and the news spread through the academy like wildfire. When we went to the cafeteria later that afternoon, many female cadets asked me if I had actually been chosen to fly with the AEB. Nobody could believe what they had heard. When in class, the instructors would call me and ask, 'Why did the CFI choose you? Did the AEB pilots ask for you to fly with them?'

Most of the male instructors had a look on their faces that meant, 'Do you really think you should be there?' All said and done, it was still a male-dominated profession. Most of the male cadets felt like I had stolen this opportunity from them, and I found myself at the receiving end of judgmental stares. Some of the senior instructors were only worried about the reputation of the academy and thought that choosing a female cadet would spoil it, since AEB pilots were known to be finicky and strict. But I had grown up in a family that had always considered both their kids to be equals. If Dada was allowed to go out for late-night parties, I, too, was never questioned when I went for one, much to the disappointment of an overprotective Dada. So this whole experience inside the academy was new to me. Even if it was just an undercurrent, I could feel its existence.

Just one day before I was to fly the sortie with the AEB, the CFI called me to his office and asked me to fly two sorties with him to brush up on my flying skills. I wanted to request the CFI to allow me to fly these two practice sorties with Babs Sir, but I couldn't, of course.

The two practice sorties were flown in the afternoon. The CFI made me revise aerobatic manoeuvres and check procedures.

The next day, I flew a sortie with Group Captain Damodaran. To my surprise, and to everyone else's, the sortie was considered to have been exceptionally well executed by the CO of AEB. There was no point given from the AEB's side after the sortie and they were all praise for the flying training branch. It was another feather in the cap of the CFI. A central briefing was organized after the AEB visit. The CFI explained what went well and what needed to be improved. Overall, the visit had been a success.

Towards the end of the briefing, the CFI mentioned that I had made the academy proud by flying one of the most perfect practice sorties with the CO of the AEB. Even the male cadets and instructors were happy and congratulated me after he had finished. For me, it was a step forward. I had been accepted among my male cadets and I was pleased with everything that had happened.

Indian military is one place that is free from any gender bias or discrimination. If I could spend the rest of my life in uniform serving in the armed forces, I would willingly do so.

TWELVE

July 1995

The second term of flight training was due to commence at the Helicopter Training School (HTS) in Hakimpet, Hyderabad. After a short break after our first term, we joined HTS in mid-July. I must mention here that HTS was entirely different from AFA in terms of training. There was no cadets' mess in HTS and we were put up in the officers' mess itself. At HTS, two cadets were asked to share a room and, as luck would have it, Anuradha and I were assigned the same room. We were elated, knowing we would get to spend two entire terms in each other's company. At HTS, we had senior cadets from the flying branch to guide us and tell us the tricks of the trade in order to survive the rigorous training sessions. Needless to say, it all came at the cost of ragda. The punishments had mellowed down quite a lot, but it was mostly because we had now learnt to avoid punishments.

Physical training was little emphasized as compared to flying and academics, where our focus had to lie. Except for PT and drill periods in the morning and afternoon, the rest of our schedule was similar to the one in AFA, with morning and afternoon flying sessions scheduled on alternate weeks. No study period was observed in the evening in HTS, but the extensive subject syllabus would compel us to study on our own. It all started with a mechanical conversion helicopter course, which went on for three weeks, followed by an exam on it, which turned out to be more difficult than the one at AFA in the previous term. A helicopter checklist is exhaustive and has a plethora of contents to learn. After this test, which came almost a month after joining the school, all the cadets were allotted instructors. I was allotted Chief Flying Instructor Wing Commander R.O.J. Assey and was his only pupil. He had recently been posted at HTS but hadn't yet joined.

As we had heard from our seniors, the start-up procedure in a helicopter was the most difficult part to learn. While other cadets had begun their training, I was waiting for the CFI to join HTS. When Anuradha would come back and tell me about how tough the start-up procedure was to understand and learn, I would worry, knowing that I was losing out while the others were learning.

I thought of seeking help and walked up to Anuradha's instructor one day. 'Who is your instructor?' he asked me. When I told him my instructor was Wing Commander Assey, he replied, 'Oh, Assey Sir? I think he should be the one to teach you about the start-up procedure, not me.' I wondered why the mention of my instructor had evoked such a reaction in him.

Anuradha advised me to speak to the flight commander who was second-in-command under the CFI. The response I received from him was no different from the last. It left me even more confused. It was after the gossip reached the other cadets that I learnt that Wing Commander Assey had the reputation of being a hard taskmaster and was known to be strict and thorough, someone who always went by the book. Why nobody wanted to teach me was because if they demonstrated anything slightly wrong to me and if the CFI later learnt about it, he would give them a hard time. Fifteen days went by and I finally knocked on the CFI's door upon his arrival. When I stepped inside, I saw in front of me a six-foot-tall, broad-built man. He was pacing up and down in his office with a bunch of documents in his hands.

'What do you want?' he asked without looking up.

'Sir, I'm your pupil, Flight Cadet Gunjan Saxena,' I answered, trying hard to sound confident.

'Okay, so you're my pupil. What have you learnt till now? Have you been to the helicopter? Have you seen the start-up?' he said, firing a volley of questions at me.

'No Sir' was all I could muster.

'Okay, let's meet tomorrow morning,' he said, and dismissed me. Although I was quite nervous to start my flying training with the CFI, I was happy it was finally going to start. The next day, I was told that the CFI was caught up with some other work and would not be able to fly. It added to my frustration as the other cadets were ahead of me in the syllabus. But when the CFI finally took me to the helicopter late in the afternoon that day, all my doubts flew out of the window. I was amazed to see him explain things with such fluency and detail. In the very first go, he taught me the rate and timing of engaging rotors, something the others had taken days to learn. I realized I was in safe hands and each lesson by Assey Sir, a thorough professional and an experienced instructor, added to my confidence.

Flying a helicopter was very different from flying a fixed wing aircraft. With extremely sensitive controls, a helicopter is inherently unstable to fly. The common mistake all cadets make initially is to give too many inputs to the controls. It takes time to understand that a helicopter is to be flown delicately, and with minimal force. One major difference between a helicopter and a fixed wing aircraft is that a helicopter has the ability to hover above one static point on the ground. As simple as it looked to us cadets, it was the most difficult thing to keep the helicopter steady in the air; it required giving continuous inputs to the controls. When cadets learn this, they tend to get tense on the controls. It happened with almost all of us and would often lead to the helicopter moving unsteadily in the air, also known to us all as an 'elephant dance'. One could easily tell by the elephant dance that a second-term cadet must be flying the helicopter at the time. Even though the CFI was known to be strict, I had begun to understand that he never raised his voice once he was inside the cockpit. His calm demeanour helped me learn the hovering part faster and better than I would have otherwise. As a result of this, I ended up performing well in the check sorties, which I flew with the commanding officer, Group Captain Sapre, who was cool, soft-spoken and relaxed. Flying with him was a welcome relief for someone who had learnt under two strict CFIs.

The only time I remember Assey Sir losing his cool with me was during the navigation phase of our training. In this phase, two pupils were to navigate using maps, and fly cross-country from one airfield to another. One pupil had to fly an onward sortie and the other the return sortie. The CFI grouped Anuradha and me together for this sortie and told me to perform well and show Anuradha a white demo. Since I had learnt quickly and thoroughly under him, complacency got the better of me and I became overconfident. Lack of preparation led me to perform one of my worst sorties in the navigation phase, so much so that Assey Sir was fuming during the entire fifty minutes of the sortie. He was so enraged in the end that he even snatched the controls from my hands. I was in tears. I knew I had let him down. Anuradha was equally confused. After the sortie was over, Assey Sir only called on Anuradha for a debriefing, while I was asked to wait outside his office. When Anuradha came out, I asked her if he had called me inside. She replied with a no. This worried me even more. When he finally came out of his office and saw me, he said, 'Do you want me to debrief you for that pathetic sortie? There's nothing I have to say. Go back and think about what you did and why you did it.' I spent the night thinking about what had gone wrong. I knew the answer, but I was not quite ready to accept it—not until the next day, when I finally told the CFI that it was the result of my lack of preparation. A long lecture followed, a lecture that shook me nice and proper, and I decided to pull up my socks after the incident.

The second term of training and the first term at HTS were drawing to an end, and a curious air of nervousness filled the air. As the final test sortie edged closer, I spent my time revising whenever and wherever possible. On the day of my final test sortie, I went to the helicopter with Group Captain Sapre. In this sortie, a cadet would be given a few exercises and one or two emergencies to handle. Group Captain Sapre gave me quite a few exercises and I performed as best as I could. Once we had almost finished the sortie and were going back for landing, Group Captain Sapre dropped a bomb.

'Tail rotor cable rupture.'

This was one of the most dreaded emergency procedures and second-term cadets were generally not told to perform it. When this emergency is called for, a cadet doesn't have rudder pedals with them any more (cadets have to take their feet off the controls), so the pitch of the tail rotor cannot be controlled.

In the absence of rudders, which control the nose of the helicopter, it becomes difficult to balance the flight. I had never imagined Group Captain Sapre would ask me to perform this emergency procedure. I knew it wasn't him making this decision. I reminded myself of all the lessons the CFI had given me, right from the beginning, and pulled off the emergency procedure after three or four attempts. Where Group Captain Sapre appreciated me for this, Assey Sir told me I had made him proud. It was all that mattered to me.

The third and final term of our training and the second term at HTS began in January 1996 after a short term break. This term was much more relaxed than the previous two, since we were now the senior-most lot in the academy. The ragda had almost died down too. But there was no respite in terms of flying and academic expectations, both of which had increased considerably. A few liberties on Sundays were the only respite for us during this term. We were allowed to go out into the city—from morning till evening. On days like these, Anuradha and I would go to Paradise Biryani, one of the most famous restaurants in Hyderabad back then, where we would eat to our heart's content. We would also get burgers packed from Burger King on our way back. Those were undoubtedly among of the better days in HTS.

Our instructors also changed in this term. Anuradha's instructor from the previous term, Wing Commander Rawat, became my instructor for this term, though I flew far less sorties with him than I did with Assey Sir, who continued to plan my sorties with him even during this term. It was my endeavour to extract all knowledge possible from Assey Sir, whose professionalism and conduct left me in awe—and still does. Things were smooth in this term and after about five months, we were sent back to the AFA Dundigal to prepare for our passing-out parade (POP).

We were back to our alma mater in the same squadrons from the first term to spend three weeks there. POP practice was on in full swing. Mornings and afternoons were spent practising and the rest of the time was whiled away in precommissioning paperwork. Exhausted from the morning parade practice, we would hardly be left with any energy to go for it again in the afternoons. The scorching heat of peak summer, mixed with the heat reflected from a metalled parade ground, would leave us drenched in sweat. Every single muscle in my body felt cramped. Though physically torturous and excruciating, POP practice was important. It was supposed to be a meticulous display of our three terms of training. The discipline learnt in training was supposed to be showcased during a synchronized parade. Each arm swing, leg stamp, turning and salute had to be practised a zillion times until it became second nature. There was no room for error. But even as we tanned our skin in the afternoon sun, there was a sense of achievement in each of us. After three terms of back-breaking training, we would finally be commissioned officers. All our hardships, each drop of sweat, seemed worthwhile in the end.

Even after three terms of training, nobody would be told their merit position until a day prior to the POP. Merit positions were based on a cadet's overall performance in flying and academics. These were disclosed during the commandant's dinner-night ceremony the night before.

All of us were very anxious that night. Even though everyone knew how they had performed, there wasn't even the slightest idea about who would make it to the top three. Apart from the top three positions, there were three other titles too: first in overall order of merit, first in flying and first in ground subjects. When the results were announced, it came as an absolute surprise to me when the commandant announced that I had won two titles, including first in overall order of merit and first in flying, apart from being first among the top three cadets. Anuradha was first in ground subjects and second among the top three cadets. Supreet stood at third position. Both of us hugged each other after the announcements. It was a coincidence that all three pupils of Babs Sir—Supreet, Anuradha and I—were among the top three. He was so happy and proud that night. I could only imagine how happy my parents would be the next day, when the reviewing officer would present the trophy to me during the parade.

It was 29 June 1996. Papaji, Maa, Dada and my friend from eleventh standard, Shivani, had come to watch the parade the next day. Papaji, who was dressed in his uniform, was told by the ushers, junior-term cadets, that their seats were reserved in the first row. Since only the parents of the trophy winners were made to sit in the first row, Papaji now had a hint of what was in store. The POP started and while marching past the reviewing officer of the parade, I stole a glance at my family. They were happy as they looked upon their marching daughter. Then came the most awaited moment. The reviewing officer started putting wings on the passing-out cadets' uniforms. These wings are considered sacred—there's a different sanctity to them. There is a saying, 'Not all the gold in the world can get you these wings, but once you have earned them, nothing in the world can take them away.' Only those who have been through flying training in the armed forces know how true this saying is. High tea was organized for the cadets and their parents after the POP. I ran straight to Papaji and saluted him—as an officer saluting another. He saluted back. It was the proudest moment of my life.

Maa was so happy she almost cried when she hugged me. 'How did such a lazy person as you manage to get this trophy?' joked Dada and hugged me. I made my parents meet Assey Sir and his wife. He even clicked our family photograph and then joined us for one. I cherish these two photographs even today. Anuradha brought her mother to meet my parents.

'So, this is it then?' she said to me while my parents were busy chatting with Anuradha's mother.

'I guess,' I said, mixed emotions taking over. 'I wish we were posted together.' Our postings had been given to us a week prior to the POP.

'I'll miss you in Bareilly,' Anuradha said with moist eyes.

'I'll miss you in Udhampur,' I replied, and we hugged each other for a long time. I wasn't aware then that the posting in Udhampur, on active duty on the front line, would test my limits of endurance.

THIRTEEN

When the postings had been disclosed, Assey Sir told me that I was being posted to one of the best stations and that I would be exposed to a variety of opportunities. After a break of three weeks, which I spent first in Delhi with my college friends and then at home in Lucknow, I headed back to Jammu, where an army convoy was waiting to take me to the Udhampur military station.

The Indian Air Force station at Udhampur was a long distance from the convoy grounds, so Flight Lieutenant Tony, who was the adjutant of my unit, had come with a Gypsy to receive me. Where I was expecting a warm welcome from my unit officer, all he said was, 'Welcome to the unit, Gunjan. Put your stuff in this Gypsy and reach the officers' mess.' After this he sat on his motorcycle and drove away. The unit did not have an independent mess and there was a common officers' mess in the air force station. Upon reaching, I met the mess manager, who told me that Srividya, my course mate who was also posted to the same unit, and I would be sharing a room on the first floor. It was a set of two rooms with a small balcony. A mess boy was assigned to us as our helper.

Srividya, a tall, lean girl, reached in the evening and we helped each other settle down. Though we hadn't talked much with each other during training, we got along quickly in no time. When we finally went outside into the beautiful garden at the mess, we could see the entire city of Udhampur, bordered by a ridgeline of green hills. Here we got a chance to speak to some of the officers of the station. But compared to the male cadets from the academy, they were almost reluctant to converse with us and were mostly cold in their behaviour, much like my unit's adjutant. We had a quiet dinner and went to our room to prepare our uniforms for the next day. The next morning after the mass briefing, we reached our unit by walking quite a distance. There was no difference in the behaviour of the unit officers there either; it was as if our presence was making them uncomfortable, and everyone was eerily quiet. Wing Commander Parab, the flight commander of the unit, took us to the commanding officer, Group Captain D'Silva, for our interview. The commanding officer was the only person we felt was warm to us and made us feel comfortable, while at the same time reiterated that our endeavour should be to learn and bring laurels to the unit by performing well, something that is expected of all young officers of any unit.

To prove our merit in our first unit, we were told to appear for a gen test to verify a pilot's knowledge about the aircraft, functioning and controls, safety procedures, etc. The test was akin to the one we had appeared for during the training. The CO even offered his old scooter to us, since commuting from the officers' mess to the unit location in the station was quite troublesome due to the long distances involved. We took the scooter from him in the evening and sat down in our room to prepare for the gen test, which was due the next morning. We performed poorly and even though we were scolded for our performance in the gen test, which we duly deserved, we were allowed to start flying. Consequently, an acceptance check sortie was scheduled on the third day, which was the first time I went airborne in that area and familiarized myself with the terrain, maps and other instructions. It was also the first time I flew in the hills.

Later that day, an officer told us that the reason the other officers were refraining from talking to us was because we were the first women pilot officers to be posted to that station, and prior to our reaching the station, all male officers were briefed to behave themselves while we were around and not get too friendly with us. Such behaviour was obvious and adjusting would require some time. And since there had never been women pilot officers in the station, the infrastructure required for women was missing as well. There were no separate changing rooms at the airstrip, so a makeshift changing room was made for the two of us using steel cupboards as a partition. One of us would stand guard while the other would change, and this happened for some time until a separate changing room was built. After about two months, I got my own blue LML Vespa. By then, the other officers had become familiar with our presence and that awkward feeling that we had sensed initially had abated.

I was often sent to ferry helicopters from the Srinagar airbase, where our unit's permanent detachment was also established. During the next two and a half years, a sense of acceptance could now be felt among other male officers of the station, and we spent a good time there. In those two years, Dada cleared his SSB, went for military training and got commissioned into the Indian Army as a second lieutenant. He began serving with a battalion of the Gorkha Rifles. Both Papaji's children were now commissioned officers.

During the same time, in 1998, India and Pakistan conducted nuclear tests, which led to an increasingly tense situation between the two countries. As a consequence, in the winter of 1998–1999, Pakistani armed forces started to send covertly trained troops of regular and paramilitary forces, allegedly in the guise of mujahideen, into Indian territory across the Line of Control (LoC). This infiltration, code-named 'Operation Badr', was aimed at severing the link between Kashmir and Ladakh, which would have caused Indian forces to withdraw from the Siachen glacier. Pakistan felt this could lead to negotiations with respect to the Kashmir dispute. But since there were no Indian troops deployed at winter-vacated posts on the Indian side, India was not aware about this infiltration. It was only on 3 May that India came to know about this, when local shepherds reported movement of Pakistani troops in the Kargil region, which was located between Kashmir and Ladakh. To confirm this, a patrol of Indian Army soldiers was sent to the hills in Kargil. The capture of five Indian soldiers, who were tortured to death, followed by heavy artillery shelling by the Pakistan Army on the ammunition dump in Kargil, revealed Pakistan's nefarious motives. In mid-May, the Indian Army mobilized more troops from Kashmir Valley to the Kargil sector.

We were unaware of these developments, since the air force was not very involved in the earlier operations. I was oblivious to the extent of operations and the gravity of the situation in the Dras–Kargil sector. In the last week of May 1999, I proceeded on leave to Lucknow. With Delhi being a transit between my journeys from Jammu to Lucknow, I spent a few days catching up with Shivani and my other friends from college. I even forgot to pay attention to the news about the Indian Air Force losing an MiG-21 fighter jet, an MiG-27 fighter jet and an Mi-17 helicopter in the last few days of May, when these were shot down by Pakistani troops. On the last day of the month, I left for Lucknow from Delhi on a night train and reached the city in the morning. Maa and Papaji had come to pick me up. Their faces were lit up with joy; so was mine. Like a happy family reunited after a long time, we went home together.

'I've cooked rajma-chawal for you,' Maa said to me as we walked towards the main door of our house.

'I'm starving, Maa, and fed up of mess food,' I said and hugged her.

'I told her to make it,' Papaji commented playfully as he unlocked the front door.

'You only ever do everything, right?' Maa shot back. Papaji stopped midway as he swung open the door to see an envelope lying on the floor.

'Oh, the postman was here!' he said and picked up the envelope.

'What does it say?' I asked. The three of us were still at the door. Papaji's eyes narrowed as he read the address mentioned on the envelope. 'It's from . . . your unit,' he said slowly as he opened it.

I was confused, but it seemed like Maa and Papaji knew what it could be.

'It's from your adjutant. It says that you have to report back to the unit immediately,' Papaji's facial expression changed from a smile to a grimace as he said this.

'But why? My leave has just started,' I said worriedly, unhappily.

'The reason is not mentioned,' Papaji said as he handed the letter to me.

'Must be an organizational requirement,' Maa added as we walked inside. 'It has happened many times in the past with your father.'

Even though I didn't take it well, my parents seemed quite okay with it. They had seen military life more than I had and were accustomed to such recall letters. It obviously saddened me and I didn't want to go.

'You must freshen up and eat your food,' Papaji said. 'In the meantime, I'll go to the Movement Control Office

(MCO) at the railway station and book a ticket for you. There's a direct train from Lucknow to Jammu.'

I spent the next few hours at home until my parents dropped me off at the railway station in the evening. Papaji asked me not to remain sad about my recall and reminded me that my duty was priority. I reached my mess at Udhampur the next evening and reported to my flight commander. He told me to meet him in the office the next morning. I remember listening to a news report that evening that said that Pakistan had started shelling NH-1, which connected Srinagar to Ladakh. It was during the next morning's briefing that I finally understood how vast the scale of this operation was. The Indian Air Force had launched Operation Safed Sagar, which was the code name assigned to the IAF's efforts to flush out Pakistani infiltrators. By the end of the first week of June, the Indian Army had recovered documents from Pakistani soldiers that proved the Pakistan Army's involvement in these infiltrations in the guise of the mujahideen. By then, my CO had already passed orders to me—I was to fly a sortie to Srinagar.

'I cannot tell you how long you will have to stay in Srinagar, but be prepared,' he said to me that evening. This was when I realized that once I had reached Srinagar, I might not be able to speak to my parents for a long time. The first thing I did after getting the order to fly to

Srinagar was ring up my parents in Lucknow from an STD booth. All I said to my parents was that I was going for some routine sorties. They asked me to take care of myself. They were undoubtedly worried, since both their children would be in the combat zone, and things were only getting worse along the LoC.

I left for Srinagar the very next day. I didn't think too much about the whole situation. To me, it was just a normal sortie, since I was accustomed to flying to the Srinagar airbase frequently. The terrain was etched in my mind. It was only when I landed at the airbase that I realized the magnitude of this war. The airbase was a madhouse, with all kinds of aircraft landing and taking off at short intervals. The crew was running haphazard on the airfield and security was increased almost ten times of the usual. Even the two rooms of our detachment were full of aircrew and our parking space was no longer reserved. I somehow managed a room for myself and stayed there for the next three days, without flying any sorties. The flying was not planned and was subject to requirement. The morning briefings were scheduled every day before sunrise, and I would attend them. A threat could be felt in the air. A war-like situation had come upon us. In the midst of this chaos, the fighter pilots and all the other male pilots had started to realize that a woman officer was in attendance among them. For many, it was strange, and nobody thought that I would be told to go further into the combat zone. To be honest, I hadn't thought of it either. In one of the briefings, I befriended Flight Lieutenant Banerjee, who was quite jovial, unlike the others, who were still hesitant. He was an ace fighter pilot who also helped me understand what had been going on in Kargil in the last few days.

When the chief operations officer (COO) of Srinagar airbase came to know about my presence there, he was not sure whether women pilot officers should be sent to the combat zone. No written policy existed at the time about women officers' role in active combat. Even then, my unit's detachment commander started planning sorties for me. My first sortie to Kargil was a reconnaissance (recce) sortie. It required flying from the Srinagar airbase and landing at the small airstrip at Kargil before going further for the recce mission. We were required to land at the Kargil airbase to be briefed by the Indian Army, based on their ground intelligence. Indian Army troops knew the ground situation better and it kept changing on an hourly basis, so a detailed briefing had become necessary. We went for the reports in a briefing room at Kargil airstrip, where we were told about the enemy's disposition, heights where our aircraft would be in direct line of the enemy's sight and, therefore, vulnerable to enemy fire and terrain, which could favour us by providing natural cover. I flew a recce sortie almost every day for the next few days. On one such day, when we were on our way to the briefing room, I saw Dada at the tarmac. Dada, dressed in his camouflage uniform, saw me at the same time. We both ran towards each other. He was shocked to see me at Kargil.

'Why are you here?' he said after he hugged me.

'I'm in Srinagar and will be flying in this area,' I replied. 'How are you, Dada?'

'I'm fine,' he said, 'but why do you have to fly in this area?'

'Why? Why should I not fly here?'

'It's not safe here,' a concerned Dada said.

'Then why are you here?' I asked. But Dada had no answer.

'It's okay, Dada, we both serve the nation,' I said, and he hugged me once more. I had met Dada after a long time. Until then, I was not aware of his deployment in the combat zone. I didn't want him to see I was worried about him. We went to the briefing room and Dada took me to have breakfast with him in his unit's temporary mess after the briefing was over. After knowing that Dada would also be coming to the same briefing room every day, we started meeting each other at the tarmac and having breakfast together over the next few days. He would tell me about the progress of the army's operations, which came at the cost of officers and men, and I would tell him about the

Air Force's involvement. I remember celebrating one morning when he told me that the Indian Army had successfully captured Tololing in Dras sector. It was a tough war, but India was slowly inching towards victory.

FOURTEEN

More than a week of tragic losses, confirmed gains and increasing tensions later, I was still flying between Kargil and Srinagar almost regularly. There was hardly any time for me to think about and realize that I was taking part in a war in the very first tenure of my service. But the second week of June was a tad less busy for me and no sorties were planned for two days straight. It was the tenth day of June, a dull and quiet day at the Srinagar airbase. Two of our four helicopters in Srinagar had gone back to Udhampur for servicing. But I was told to stay in Srinagar. The day started with the regular morning briefing, where I came to know about a fighter mission that would take place in the morning. Another thing that was being talked about by everyone was how Pakistan, as a 'goodwill gesture', had, on 3 June, released Flight Lieutenant K. Nachiketa, an Indian Air Force pilot taken as a prisoner of war by the Pakistan Army patrol on 27 May 1999, when his MiG-27 had crashed. But there was news of the handing over of mutilated bodies of six soldiers of a battalion of the JAT regiment. Where was goodwill or the spirit of soldiering in that? There were rumours everywhere about how Pakistan was treating captured soldiers. After hearing what they did to the six soldiers of the JAT regiment, officers and men of the Indian Air Force started discussing how it would be better to just shoot oneself rather than become a prisoner of war if their aircraft crashed into enemy territory. I would not deny that this thought crossed my mind that day. After all, I had been flying over captured hostile territory and the possibility of getting caught did exist. The rest of the day was spent in doing almost nothing. Sitting alone in a small room on a rather quiet afternoon, I began to imagine how I would put my INSAS rifle to use if I ever got caught. 'Whatever happens, I will not let them capture me alive'—I had somehow made a silent pact with myself somewhere in the back of my mind, even though I tried to shrug off any thoughts about it. Listening to the news on the radio about how France and the United States had acknowledged that Pakistan was responsible for crossing the LoC, I slipped into a deep slumber.

Have you ever travelled in a train for so long that when you finally get off at your destination, you can still feel the ground beneath your feet shaking the same way as on a moving train? A feeling similar to this made me wake up from my sleep, but it was not related to trains. I thought I heard muffled sounds of blasts and distant gunfire. When I got out of bed and walked outside, there was a strange silence on the airstrip. I had been hearing the sounds of blasts and gunfire so much on my regular visits to Kargil that I felt like I could hear them even in my sleep. It was a strange feeling. When inside the briefing room at Kargil or just flying over enemy bunkers, I could hear the muffled sounds of artillery bombardment only a few hundred metres from us, sounds of machine-gun fire echoing in the valleys or, at times, could see muzzle flashes in the rocky mountains, which would make me realize all over again that a bloody battle was underway somewhere in those mountains. But it all creeps into the subconscious even if no attention is paid to it. Sometimes I would be taking a nap inside the mess before a sortie, and suddenly the sound of mortar fire or artillery gunfire would wake me up. Sometimes these mortar rounds would go off so close to the airstrip that we could feel the windowpanes vibrating. But nothing mattered in that moment. The battle noise was not discomforting—it was the silence that was dreadful.

As I stood outside my room in the sunny afternoon, I could see that a wreath-laying ceremony was going on in a far corner of the airstrip. Men in army and air force uniforms slowly marched towards a row of coffins covered in tricolour carrying the mortal remains of martyred soldiers from the night before or that morning, and offered wreaths to the martyrs as the buglers played a tune. The battle had ended for these bravehearts. They would now be airlifted to their hometowns, where their grieving families awaited them for their last rites. I wondered in that moment if their families were even aware of this or whether they would be told later. I had never found the time to think about this before that day, even though I had been witnessing these ceremonies since I had come to Srinagar. War is surely a sad affair in the end. The enemy held defences at heights and was, therefore, at an advantage. And at the very beginning of the war, Indian troops were fighting in what appeared to be suicide missions, as the army had not yet achieved a considerable build-up of forces. But then it reminded me of Papaji's words, who always considered martyrdom a privilege. There was no better way to die, he would say, and that all of us should be proud of them. Only the most fortunate get to live and die as heroes; only the most fortunate get to be wrapped in tricolour. No ordinary man could earn it.

I felt respect and grief for the martyrs at the same time as I stood witness to the wreath-laying ceremony from a distance. I closed my eyes and paid homage to all those who had laid down their lives for their nation since the Kargil War had begun.

Since 6 June 1999, the army had achieved a sufficient build-up of troops and the logistics to launch major offences in the Dras and Kargil sectors. The war was only going to intensify in the coming days. And it would be accompanied by strategic air strikes, since the aim was to keep the Srinagar–Leh highway free of enemy threat. One such air strike was carried out earlier that day. As I stood there lost in my thoughts, our flight commander, Wing Commander Srivastav, came running towards me.

'Good afternoon, Sir,' I saluted him.

He saluted back as he stopped in front of me, catching his breath. 'We need to hurry up,' he said. 'We need to get airborne immediately.'

'Where are we going?' I asked.

'Kargil,' he replied.

'Now?' I had to ask. Sunset was edging closer as we spoke. To prepare the helicopter, to add fuel to it, get clearances for flying and go to Kargil and then come back was a lot to do in this little time.

'There was an air strike at the enemy supply dumps and a few posts this morning. Damage assessment needs to be done. The army can't go there, since the enemy is sitting at a higher altitude. So we have been asked to do it.'

He paused for a while, looked at his wristwatch and said, 'Sunset is only three hours away. Meet me in the briefing room. We're racing against time.'

This recce sortie was the need of the hour. Wing Commander Srivastav told me and the other male pilot during the briefing that the army was supposed to launch further offensives the next morning with the aim of capturing Tololing, and all plans for these would depend on the degree of damage caused by the air strikes. The Tololing Top, a dominant position overlooking the Srinagar–Leh highway (NH-1D), was a vital objective, the capture of which could change the course of war. And if not fought off, the enemy could cut off the army's only supply route to Kargil. Since the start of the Battle of Tololing on 20 May 1999, we had lost many soldiers, including air force personnel. An Mi-17 helicopter was shot down on 28 May near Tololing by a Pakistani surface-to-air missile, which had resulted in the martyrdom of four air warriors.

The helicopter we were flying was not clear to fly in the hills after sunset. And the sun in the hills sets earlier than in the plains, owing to the terrain. As per rules, in plains, a pilot is supposed to land half an hour prior to sunset, and only if he/she is flying at their base where they're familiar with the terrain, are they given a special clearance to fly until sunset. Since Srinagar was not our base, we had to land half an hour prior to sunset, and that, too, after hill correction time was added to it. This left us with less than three hours to perform our recce.

Of the male pilot and me, the flight commander asked me to be his co-pilot that evening. I was sincerely hoping for him to choose me as I didn't want to sit there whiling away time and overthinking.

'Gunjan, you run and get the clearances and draw weapons; we'll prepare the helicopter,' the flight commander ordered after he had finished the briefing. Since it was a non-flying day, we had not even drawn our rifles and pistols from the armoury. I sprinted to the Gypsy and went straight to the office to get clearances. I dashed to the armoury after that and got our weapons. When I reached the helicopter after getting the required documents and weapons, the flight commander was already there talking on a landline.

'The sanitization report has not reached yet,' the flight commander said after hanging up. There was a sense of urgency in his voice. 'It doesn't matter; you go ahead with the start-up. And I want a fast start-up.'

Everything was in fast-forward mode that evening. I followed the fast start-up procedure, in which a pilot is required to perform all necessary checks but needs to expedite them considerably to save time. I could see from the cockpit that a jittery flight commander was pacing up and down near the telephone. I contacted the air traffic control (ATC) on radio to ask for permission to start up, which was denied since a sanitization report was pending. In Kargil, if a pilot had to go for a sortie at that time, the army had to sanitize that particular area, and a sanitization report had to be obtained before a sortie could be flown in that area. This was to ensure there was no grave threat to the aircraft.

I went ahead with the start-up anyway and convinced the ATC that I would not engage the rotors until the sanitization report reached us. Seeing that I was adamant and would not back down, the ATC did not say anything. The flight commander got into the helicopter and strapped himself to the seat. Even in this cold weather both of us were sweating. Our overalls were drenched.

'The sanitization report is still pending,' he said. 'What do we do now?'

Every second of delay put our mission in graver danger of jeopardy. The failure of this mission could result in casualties the next day. Lack of damage assessment could compromise plans. I did not want any of it to happen. Nobody should have to die because a sortie had failed due to a delayed sanitization report, I thought.

I looked at the flight commander, engaged the rotors and said, 'Let's get airborne, Sir.'

The ATC kept asking me to disengage and wait. I kept telling them that we would only get airborne and wait for the sanitization report before entering the combat zone. Technically, we weren't breaking any rules, only bending them a little. But this would save us time. At least my flight commander was convinced. Soon, we were in the air and headed towards Kargil. As luck would have it, the ATC informed us before we entered the combat zone that the sanitization report had reached them and that we could go ahead. The flight commander looked at me, and we both smiled as our helicopter headed towards its mission.

The recce sortie was carried out and we were able to return to the Srinagar airstrip on time. Our damage-assessment report was submitted to the higher headquarters. The dull start to the day had ended with an adrenaline rush. The takeaway was that things could change in war in no time. Orders could come anytime from anywhere, and they had to be followed. The mission was the priority, and with a little ingenuity, one could accomplish the mission against all odds. But rules had to be followed even during the hardest times. Procedures that were set in place over years of experience had a purpose and they should never be bypassed. Discipline was the key to soldiering.

I cannot say for sure how much our report helped the higher headquarters but such small reports from all departments must have helped in getting a glimpse of the bigger picture. The air force was playing its role so well that on 12 June 1999, the Pakistani foreign minister Sartaj Aziz hastily arrived in New Delhi and implored India to stop the air strikes. Finally, in the next two days, after a coordinated effort by the air force and the army, the difficult posts on the icy slopes of Tololing were captured. Tololing was won on 13 June 1999. It changed the course of the war thereafter.

FIFTEEN

21 June 1999

Pakistan had faced enough humiliation and was on the verge of losing the war, but was still adamant about not withdrawing its troops from Kargil, even when pressurized by the then president of the United States of America, Bill Clinton. India, on the other hand, had won one hard-earned victory after another while so many martyrs registered their respectful names in the history of the nation. Heroes emerged on the battlefield every day. In the making were exemplary stories of valour that would inspire successors for generations to come.

The war in Kargil had taught me a few lessons as well. I had understood the importance of life and what we must make of it before time ran out. I was making the best of my life while in Srinagar, learning lessons of discipline, determination, improvisation and ethics on the front line. And yet there was so much more waiting for me.

Eight pilots from my unit, including me, had stationed themselves in Srinagar since the war had begun. As the only female officer in the group, our detachment commander, who was also the flight commander, felt responsible for my well-being under his command. He would keep asking me if I needed anything and urged me to not hesitate in telling him if there was anything that made me uncomfortable. Thinking that I might get uncomfortable at times, he would refrain from sending me on sorties to unknown, isolated locations in the combat zone against my will. Little did he know that he could refrain only until I was the only option left for him.

The flight commander, Wing Commander Srivastav, explained the schedule for the next morning as we were about to sit down for dinner in the dining hall of our detachment. There was a planned communication sortie the next morning and the flight commander, along with another pilot, had to ferry a passenger in his helicopter to a helipad in the forward area; I, along with another pilot in the second helicopter, was supposed to accompany him as his back-up. So it was going to be a simple sortie the next day. The third helicopter of our detachment was supposed to stay in Srinagar with the other pilots, in case any contingency mission came up. After the briefing was over, we sat for dinner.

It was in the middle of our meal that an airman came with a message for the flight commander that the chief operations officer (COO) wanted to speak to him urgently. For a while there was silence around the table, with everyone contemplating what emergency it could possibly be. Such messages always brought anxiety in those days. The flight commander came back and informed us that there was a slight change in the schedule for the next morning. But this change wasn't going to be altogether comforting, especially for me. A sortie had been planned for casualty evacuation from a helipad very close to the LoC in the Uri sector, the flight commander informed us.

'But it isn't as simple as it sounds,' he added.

'Why, Sir?' one of our fellow pilots asked. But only I had an idea what the flight commander was concerned about.

'It's the helipad,' he said as he stirred his daal.

'Too close to the LoC,' another pilot said, 'but we've been to helipads close to the LoC. We know the drill.'

'Have you been to this one?' the flight commander asked, still not eating the food on his plate.

'No, Sir,' came a swift reply.

'Has anyone here been to this helipad?' a worried flight commander asked.

'I have, Sir,' I said, a few seconds after nobody answered. Suddenly, all heads turned towards me.

'Gunjan, please tell the others about this helipad,' he instructed.

'Navigating to this helipad is quite challenging,' I started. 'The valley is quite confusing. There are too many turns and you cannot simply follow the bends of the river below you or the features around you to get there.'

Everyone listened to me quietly, even the flight commander. 'No sortie is permitted to that helipad if the pilot and the co-pilot have not been there before. Even on occasions that either the pilot or the co-pilot has been there, the pilots have got confused. Their helicopters crossed the LoC and had to be directed back.'

'So I guess Gunjan will have to switch then,' one of the pilots said.

One thing was sure, and all of us knew it, that I would have to switch with the pilot who was scheduled to wait at the Srinagar airbase the next day for any contingency. There was nobody else among the eight of us who had been to this helipad in the Uri sector before. The flight commander's sortie was an important one, so he couldn't have gone with me for this casevac (casualty evacuation). The army had just captured Point 5140, the last objective on Tololing peak. And a VIP, who was supposed to visit there, was the flight commander's passenger. So the next senior pilot, Wing Commander Joshi, was assigned as the captain of the casevac sortie. But the flight commander had still not said anything about my switching. For a moment I felt that he was concerned about sending a female officer to a mission so dangerous. His concern was valid, since he was responsible for my well-being.

'Do you still remember the valley's terrain?' a concerned flight commander asked.

'I remember, Sir,' I said, trying to sound confident even when I was worried inside. 'Don't worry, Sir, I will not disappoint you.'

'All right, so it's decided. You go get some sleep. You have to take off at first light,' said the flight commander, and went back to eating his dinner.

I started sweating about this newly assigned responsibility as I walked to my room. There were no GPS devices in those days, so pilots had to familiarize themselves with the map and the actual terrain for navigation. Scenes from the previous sortie to this helipad started flashing in front of my eyes. But more than a year had passed, and it was all too blurry. I had assured the flight commander for two reasons—it was a casevac, so someone's life was at stake, and it was also an opportunity for me to prove myself.

No sooner had I entered my room than I took out the map of the valley and started going through it carefully. When I had gone to this helipad before, I had gone with a senior pilot who had earlier been there. The responsibility of navigation had not fallen to me then. And there was no war going on back then. If one crossed the LoC now, things could get worse. After all the necessary preparations on the map were done, I went to sleep. I had to wake up fresh the next day. But even after a while, I felt myself struggling to sleep as thoughts about what could go wrong flooded my mind. It was then that I remembered what the captain of my previous sortie to this helipad had taught me—something that would hold me in good stead the next day.

There was a particular turn in this valley where pilots usually got confused. The key to not getting confused was timing. In flying, when a pilot takes off he/she is supposed to bring the aircraft to a particular height and then set the course at a constant speed. This constant speed and distance to the helipad could be used to calculate the time it would take to reach that confusing turn to avoid any trouble. Since the flying distance to that helipad was not much, the time required for this calculation was also very less. But now I knew what I had to do. Soon, I fell asleep.

The next day I woke up even before the alarm went off. I prepared myself for the sortie and went to the helicopter. This mission had no margin for error. No time for a recce would be available once airborne and the luxury of hovering over the area to spot the helipad was not there due to its location very close to the LoC.

'All the best, Gunjan. Do everything right,' Flight Lieutenant Kagti, who was the only officer there with the same seniority as mine, said to me as he walked past me to the helicopter that I was supposed to fly earlier. He was the one I had switched with.

'I don't know, I'm just nervous,' I said.

'You weren't trained to be nervous,' he said, and smiled before getting into the cockpit. I replied with a bleak smile. But he was right. I wasn't trained to let nervousness jeopardize a mission. I did not pass out from the academy with flying colours just to get nervous. I was very much capable of pulling it off, I assured myself. With this as a reminder, I got inside the cockpit as soon as the captain arrived.

'I hope your photographic memory serves you well today. Now let's get to the start-up procedure,' the captain said, as he strapped himself to his seat. He noticed that I was a bit shaky in my start-up procedure. He could see that I was still nervous. And there was no denying that I was.

And then we took off. We orbited over Srinagar to gain height up to 5000 feet for vertical clearance from small arms fire or shoulder-fired missiles. During the climb, I mentally shook myself and told myself I couldn't be jittery about this any more. Pulling myself together, I took out the map, took the bearings, did my calculations for timing based on the ground speed, adjusted our ETA and switched on the stopwatch to ensure I did not overshoot our position. As per standard operating procedure, if we failed to spot our helipad by the calculated time, we were to return without completing the casevac, because hovering was prohibited in that area due to the dangers involved. And I did not want to deprive a casualty of a chance at getting proper medical aid. The life of a soldier was at stake, and I did not want to fail. I was responsible for navigating and finding the helipad. Failing to do so, I would be held responsible for the unsuccessful sortie and my experience of flying in this area would go in vain. Not only this, my flight commander's faith in me would be shaken.

As we entered the valley, I concentrated only on the navigation. After only a few minutes, the stopwatch indicated that the turn had come. But I couldn't identify it as I looked down at the valley, and it made me nervous. Nevertheless, I was confident that I had calculated the timing right, so I took the turn.

'I can't spot the helipad, can you?' the captain asked.

I desperately scanned the area below to see if I could spot it. As per the stopwatch, only thirty seconds were left to reach the destination and if we didn't spot the helipad, we would have to turn around and go back.

'There it is!' I exclaimed joyfully as smoke from the smoke candles became visible. Smoke candles were lit by the army near the helipad to help us spot it. I finally relaxed. My captain relaxed too. A sense of achievement pumped inside me.

Smoke swirled under the powerful rotors of our helicopter and waves of dust swept across the helipad as we descended. As soon as we landed and signalled the team there, stretcher bearers ran towards the helicopter with the casualty. The rotors were kept engaged, since time was of the essence. We took off as soon as the stretcher bearers got to a safe distance away from us. A major-ranked officer in charge of that unit smiled at us and gave us a thumbs up as he stood at the edge of the helipad clad in his worn-out dungarees. I smiled back, and flew away from the valley.

The mission had been a success and I couldn't wait to see the look on my flight commander's face. I hadn't let him down. I was happy that even with less than three years of service, I had been considered for such a difficult sortie and I had pulled it off.

With India slowly emerging victorious in this war, a sulking Pakistan Army was trying to cause maximum damage to the Indian side, and its ill intentions led to an incident that shook me to such an extent that I was left scared for the first time since the war had begun.

SIXTEEN

Air Chief Marshal Birender Singh Dhanoa (Param Vishisht Seva Medal, Ati Vishisht Seva Medal, Yudh Seva Medal, Vayu Sena Medal and Aide-De-Camp), the twenty-fifth chief of the air staff of the Indian Air Force from December 2016 to September 2019, addressed a gathering of pilots at the Indian Women Pilots' Association conference in Delhi three years ago. Srividya and I were invited to the conference and the air chief marshal reminisced about the one time he had been a passenger in a Cheetah helicopter flown by me.

June 1999

Wing Commander B.S. Dhanoa, a fighter pilot who was commanding a fighter squadron in Srinagar, had come on board my helicopter for an aerial recce of the forward area in Kargil. We were supposed to land in Kargil for an intelligence briefing before flying ahead. Dada came to know that I was arriving for the briefing, so he came to the tarmac to receive me.

'We've captured two peaks near Tiger Hill,' Dada exclaimed happily as he walked towards me on the tarmac.

'Congratulations to the army,' Wing Commander Dhanoa said to him as he got down from the helicopter. That's when Dada saw him and saluted. He saluted back.

'Sir,' I intervened to introduce them to each other, 'he's Captain Anshuman Saxena, my elder brother.' The officer seemed a little surprised as he shifted his gaze from Dada to me, and then back to Dada.

'So both siblings are here in Kargil?' an astonished Wing Commander Dhanoa asked. Dada and I nodded. 'You must have anxious parents back at home.'

It was when he said this that I realized how worried Papaji and Maa would be. It wouldn't have been easy for them to spend each day knowing that both their kids were participating in the war.

But for Kargil, it was just another sortie, and Dada and I had just come out of the briefing room. Dada insisted on walking me to my helicopter, since I was supposed to return to Srinagar later that day.

'Were you able to speak to Maa and Papaji?' he asked.

'Not since I left Udhampur,' I said, 'but I've written to them.'

'And I haven't been able to find time to do even that,' Dada said.

'Do you miss them?' I asked deliberately, knowing that Dada wouldn't display any emotions to his younger sister.

'Don't *you* miss them?' Dada asked back, smartly evading the question. But both of us could see the concern. Before I could say anything, I noticed the lines deepening on Dada's forehead as he seemed to try to listen to something. As did all the other men around us. Within a split second, a faint whistling reached my ears as well.

'Gunjan, run!'

A frantic Dada pulled me by the arm as he started to run. Everybody had dispersed to either side of the tarmac. Dada dashed inside a bunker, and I followed. Everything happened so quickly that I didn't have time to understand what was going on. It was when I looked out from the bunker's loophole that I realized that a missile had landed and exploded just a few metres from my helicopter—the whistling sound was the missile propelling through the air. My ears rang from the explosion. For a while, I couldn't hear anything but my heartbeat, which was faster than normal. It was at this very moment that I saw fear on Dada's face. He wasn't afraid for his life; he was afraid for *me.* He was holding on to my hand tightly and screaming, 'Are you stupid? Why didn't you run? Didn't you hear the missile coming?'

How would I have known it was a missile? It was the first time I had experienced something like this. In that moment I realized the uncertainty of life during war.

Since the airstrip at Kargil was out of the direct line of sight of any of the Pakistani-occupied bunkers, they could only target it by listening to the sounds of the aircraft landing and taking off. Their intent was to cause damage to the aircraft and wreak havoc among the Indian ranks. Before the Pakistanis could target our helicopter again, my captain and I rushed to it and took off in a hurry. The Pakistani troops attempted such shelling in the future as well—but without success.

This incident wasn't the end of such experiences for me. When flying close to the LoC, we were always briefed on which route to take and which of the enemy bunkers could attack us with shoulder-fired missiles. To counter the possibility of an attack, we had two options in front of us. We could either fly using the cover of the ridgeline or maintain an elevation of more than 5000 feet. I would take the second option, since a recce sortie required observation in the enemy area, and it wasn't possible while flying using cover. After one such sortie, the captain of my helicopter and I were called by the COO to his office. It had to be something of concern, since the COO wouldn't just call junior officers without reason. We wondered if we had done something wrong. When we were waiting outside his office, the COO's runner told us he had called me inside first.

'May I come in, Sir?' I asked as I saluted him. Sitting behind a big walnut-wood table in his camouflage uniform, he gestured to me to come inside.

'Yes, you, young lady,' he said in his heavy, commanding voice. 'Do you know where you flew today?'

'Yes, Sir,' I said. 'We flew over the Dras sector and came back.'

'Can you mark the route on the map and tell me?' he said, looking at me with his index finger pointing at a blow-up of the Dras–Kargil sector map that hung on the wall behind his chair.

'Yes, Sir,' I said and walked towards the wall. I ran my index finger along the surface, tracing my flight path.

'Do you know you were flying over enemy bunkers?' the COO asked.

'Yes, Sir.'

'Do you know that a volley of missiles was fired towards your helicopter?'

'No, Sir,' I said, surprised at what he had just told me.

'You barely escaped,' he said. 'The missiles went off a few metres below your helicopter. The ground formation passed this intelligence report to me.'

I did not know what to say, so I kept quiet.

'What if one of them had hit you?' he asked.

'I was doing my duty, Sir.' It was all I could say.

'How many recce sorties have you flown till now?' he asked.

'I do not remember exactly, Sir,' I answered. 'But I think . . . around forty.'

'All recce sorties by the air force contribute towards disclosing enemy disposition,' he continued. 'So you're adding to better planning and strategies by our own forces by discharging your duties fearlessly and sincerely. I am proud of young officers like you. I wish you godspeed and good luck.'

This encounter with the COO left me thinking about life and death. It was the second time I had felt fear. I do not feel ashamed to admit it. But I made sure not to let it get to me. Hundreds of bullets would have been fired at my helicopter during all my sorties, hundreds of missiles would have targeted me, but I did not think about it at all. A fully loaded INSAS assault rifle and a revolver in my helicopter would often remind me that I might be taken as a prisoner of war if my helicopter crashed behind enemy lines. But I continued to do what I was supposed to. The chaos of war doesn't allow you to overthink, only act. There is no place for thoughts, only orders. And I was busy following orders. It was all I had learnt to do. It is all that is taught to any soldier.

Besides, what I had primarily learnt during this war was the value of time and life. Evacuation of casualties from the front line would often become part of my sorties. I remember one such casualty evacuation quite distinctly.

We had just dropped some supplies and passengers from Srinagar to Kargil. On our way back, the captain received a radio call asking him to take a detour, since a soldier who had been severely injured had to be evacuated urgently. Upon receiving the coordinates for the helipad, we redirected our helicopter towards the given location. But by the time we reached, the soldier had succumbed to his injuries. A bullet had hit his head, we were told.

The officer-in-charge in that location asked the captain if we could carry the mortal remains of the soldier to Srinagar. He asked me if I would be comfortable with it, since the body would be strapped to the passenger seat, there being no space for a coffin inside the small cabin of our Cheetah helicopter. I told him that it was the least we could do for the martyred soldier. But the entire process of getting his mortal remains to the helicopter and then carefully placing the body on the passenger seat did shake me up.

I felt a sort of grief that is inexplicable. Seeing his head wrapped in a cloth and his uniform crimsoned with blood was something that made me wonder if this soldier had experienced a lot of pain. *What would have been his last thoughts? How would his parents react when they were told their son was no more? Was he married? Did he have children? What about all the plans he must have had for the future?* Such questions roiled inside my head until we landed at the Srinagar airbase. But such is the uncertainty of a soldier's life, I reminded myself. There is glory in fighting to save the integrity of one's nation and dying in the process. A death like this is earned by fortunate men and women. I saluted the martyr and vowed to myself that I would honour the supreme sacrifice of all martyrs of war by doing my duty undauntedly. This kept me going till the end of the war.

In the second week of July, a victorious mood could be felt everywhere. It was a decisive victory for the Indian troops, which had been successful in drawing out the infiltrators and recapturing vital peaks. But it had all come at the cost of loading tens of coffins every day. Nevertheless, their sacrifice had not been futile. The war officially came to an end when the Indian Army announced the complete eviction of Pakistani intruders on 26 July 1999. Prime Minister Atal Bihari Vajpayee declared Operation Vijay, the Indian Army's operation to push back infiltrators in the Kargil War, a success on 14 July 1999.

After the Kargil operations were over, a static display of all aircraft that had participated in the war was organized at the tarmac of the Srinagar airbase for the press and the media. No cameras were allowed and reporters were asked to use recorders only. So the reporters started interviewing pilots standing in front of their aircraft. After a while, a bunch of reporters started to gather about me as I stood in front of my Cheetah helicopter, the smallest flying machine on the tarmac that day. Soon, the crowd of reporters in front of me started to grow bigger. It was only after one of the reporters pointed this out that I realized that I was the only woman pilot on the tarmac—the only woman pilot to have flown in the combat zone during Kargil operations.

'Our fighter jets and huge transport aircraft failed to attract the media the way Gunjan's little Cheetah did today at the tarmac,' the other pilots joyfully commented later in the evening during a mess function.

It was a wonderful feeling to land back in Udhampur—there was both achievement and pride. All my unit officers had gathered on the tarmac to welcome us. I could see a broad smile on the face of my CO. The men of my unit shook hands with me as they welcomed me with a smile, the same men who had been hesitant to follow my orders or help me in preparations of my sortie back when I had just joined. It took going to a war to earn this respect. I cherished every moment of it.

What war teaches you in a few days cannot be learnt in an entire lifetime. But then again, nobody should get to learn things the way one learns during a war. Young men and women willingly sign their wills when they join the armed forces without thinking about the uncertainty of their lives, but war puts this thought before all others in their head.

Serving away from home and fighting in rough terrain is not the only price paid by soldiers defending the territorial integrity of their nation. The sounds of exploding bombs and ricocheting bullets remain in their memories, often waking them up from sleep. Insomnia, stress and anxiety are the unsaid, unavoidable ghosts that stay even after the war has ended. Those who understand the value of the uniform of the Indian military and the responsibility that comes with it will continue to strive to earn it—for it offers a respectful life, a life full of adventure, a life less ordinary.

It has been more than two decades since I participated in the Kargil War, but its memories are still fresh in my mind. The lessons I learnt during that time have been the guiding beacons that help me take decisions even today. I understand the value of family better, I respect time more than before and I carry a sense of gratitude within me for every moment of my life I get to spend happily. Even though I have retired from the Indian Air Force, its ethos will forever remain in my heart. I was, I am and I will remain a flight lieutenant, the rank that is the most valuable thing I've earned in this lifetime.

AFTERWORD

So that was how my journey was till Kargil. And what a journey it was—full of tough times, challenges, opportunities and adventures. There were times when I felt on top of the world and also when I wanted to give up, when I had doubts about myself. My heart and mind were seldom on a separate page but on every such occasion, I was able to align them in overcoming obstacles. To sum up, it was a journey full of learning.

Post Kargil, my life traversed a different path. I was posted to a helicopter unit in the North-east sector, which proved extremely lucky for me. There, I met my perfect match. I got married to Wing Commander Gautam Narain, a helicopter pilot of the Indian Air Force. We were blessed with a daughter, Pragya. She brought so much happiness into our world, which we never knew existed. Gautam and I started enjoying the roller-coaster ride that is parenthood. After my daughter was born, I decided to hang up my uniform. But, fortunately, my association with the Indian Air Force continued—as the spouse of an officer.

Even without adorning a uniform or occupying a cockpit, I felt part of the air force. I continued to interact with young officers and saw a positive change in their outlook—the whole organization was evolving and changing progressively towards accepting female officers. It has been a pleasure to witness the gradual change in the work profiles of female officers. It is heartening to see them hold key operational posts in the Indian Air Force, which we could only dream of when we joined the organization.

A frequently asked question to me, which I love to answer, is how I feel after having retired.

I cherish every single minute that I spent serving in the air force. Irrespective of how I felt while going through it, each experience, big or small, has made me what I am today. During my association with the air force, I came across a whole lot of amazing people. I made some great friends, with whom I now share a bond for life. They have stood by me through thick and thin. Even though I don't adorn the air force uniform any longer, what has become an inseparable part of my personality are the ethos and values imbibed from the thorough and professional training I received when I was part of the air force. The training and experiences I have had have helped me evolve as a stronger and more confident individual. And it is this mental strength that has helped me on several occasions to sail through tough and trying times.

On the domestic front, as I slipped into the role of a full-time housewife, it dawned upon me very soon that it wasn't as simple as I had thought. It took me some time and effort to learn to manage the household chores, along with my daughter and my pets. Here the experienced 'better halves' of the male officers came to my rescue. And soon I learnt all the tricks of the trade from them!

I do sincerely hope that readers will enjoy reading my story, as much as Captain Nirvan, Mr Kirandeep and I have enjoyed writing it for them.

If this book is able to inspire even one small-town girl to pursue her dream against all odds, I would feel the effort writing this has been worth it. Thank you for your patient reading.

Jai Hind!

ACKNOWLEDGEMENTS

Sometimes life throws some very unexpected and pleasant surprises our way—this book is certainly one of them.

When I participated in the Kargil operations, I didn't have the faintest idea that it would get me the nickname 'The Kargil Girl'. As work for the motion picture was coming to an end, I got a call from Nirvan Singh one evening. He told me about the idea of the book, but I was not very sure about writing it. I agreed primarily on seeing his enthusiasm and conviction about the project. As work on the book began, I realized I had made the right decision. I would like to thank both Nirvan and Kiran for not only encouraging and supporting me through the writing of the book, but also for always being extremely patient and understanding.

Acknowledgements

Thanks are due to Suhail Mathur, for all his help and efforts in making this project successful.

To my publisher Penguin Random House India and the commissioning editor Gurveen Chadha, for all the support.

To my instructors Group Captain Sanjeeb Kumar Barbora, Group Captain Subash Shankar Rao Patil, Air Commodore R.O.J. Assey and Air Commodore Mukesh Rawat (the order in which they taught me), whom I can never thank enough. Whatever I am today was made possible because of their teachings, guidance and encouragement.

To the Indian Air Force, for helping me realize my dream of flying in the blue skies, and for all the opportunities I got. It has been an honour and a privilege to serve in this magnificent organization. My sincere thanks to my commanding officer and my flight commander during the Kargil operations.

My biggest gratitude to Maa and Papaji. I would not have reached anywhere had it not been for their love and unconditional support and blessings. My brother has been my toughest competition (who always made me stretch my limits), my friend, my critic, my supporter, my partner in crime and so much more.

To my partner for life, Wing Commander Gautam Narain, the only reason I am able to juggle the different roles and responsibilities in my life.

Acknowledgements

To my lucky charm, my daughter Pragya, who brings zeal and freshness to my life every single day. I feel so blessed to have you.

—Flt Lt Gunjan Saxena (retd)

I was very young when the Kargil War broke out. I remember I used to see convoys of military transport vehicles going up and down NH-44 back in 1999, when I used to live at my grandmother's house in Udhampur. I would often ask my father about the movement of these large convoys. It was then that my father explained to me the concept of battles and wars, and told me that our country was fighting one. It was during these days that I heard the name 'Flight Lieutenant Gunjan Saxena' on one of the news channels. Little did I know that I would be writing about her one day. But when I started learning about military history back in 2016, I deemed it important to write about the war heroes of this country. 'Flight Lieutenant Gunjan Saxena' happened to be the first name that came to mind. Many a man has been glorified, and deservingly so. But I felt that very little was available about the contribution of women to this country's battles and wars. So the idea to co-write Gunjan Ma'am's autobiography was very thrilling.

At the outset, I would like to thank Flight Lieutenant Gunjan Saxena (retd) for trusting me with the responsibility of writing about her life. She has been very humble, kind and helpful, and her professionalism and discipline have helped us match all deadlines on time. Being co-authors of her autobiography is a singular honour, and it has been our endeavour to tell readers about how wonderful a person she is, besides being a woman in uniform, a loving daughter and a sister, a caring wife and a responsible mother.

My heartfelt thanks to my literary agent, Suhail Mathur, for pushing me to write this book and motivating me at every step.

I would like to thank Penguin Random House India and my commissioning editor Gurveen Chadha for believing in our work and being patient with us while we wrote the book. Gurveen's relentless efforts have helped this book take better shape than how we had written it.

I would like to thank my co-author, Kirandeep Singh, for being by my side in all our literary endeavours.

I sincerely thank Lieutenant Colonel Abhishek for connecting me to Gunjan Ma'am. I would also like to thank my commanding officers Colonel Yogesh, Lieutenant Colonel Saikat, Lieutenant Colonel Rajendra and Colonel K.J., along with all my fellow officers and

course mates, for supporting my passion for writing.[*]
I thank Gauravjit for going out of the way to help me
during the final stage of writing this book.

Lastly, I would like to thank my Nani, Didi and Jiju,
my parents, Aarushi, Rohan, and my fur babies Scooby
and Sultan for their unconditional support and love.

—Nirvan Singh

Kargil—the name itself takes me back to the days I used
to listen to the news about India's war against infiltrators.
Casualties were reported every day and many young officers
sacrificed their lives for the nation. Captain Sourabh Kalia
and Captain Vikram Batra's faces are still etched in my
mind. Many documentaries and films have been made on
the Kargil War but I, as a writer, always wanted to contribute
to the cause of glorifying the deeds of these bravehearts in
writing. This motivated me to co-write the autobiography
of Flight Lieutenant Gunjan Saxena (retd)—'The Kargil
Girl'. I am thankful to her for trusting us to give words to
her story.

I couldn't have dreamt about writing this book if my
co-author, Nirvan, hadn't been there with me.

---

[*] All full names withheld.

Acknowledgements

I thank Suhail Mathur of The Book Bakers and Penguin Random House India for giving us this opportunity.

My sincere thanks to all my family members, especially Jiwan Jyoti Phul and Pavitdeep Singh Phul, my friends Gursahib Singh, Bhupinder Singh, Vikas Mittal, Ranjit Singh, Harbir Singh and Nakul Malik, and confidante Rabia Arora for their constant support.

Lastly, I would like to thank my late furry friend Shaggy. You're still my 'good boy'.

—Kirandeep Singh